My First Crush

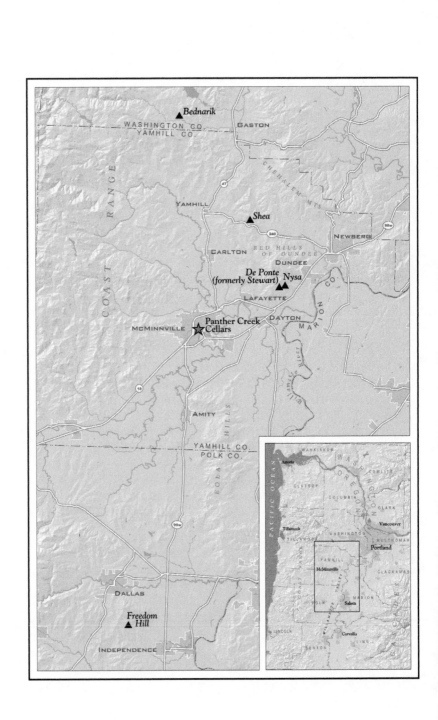

My First Crush

MISADVENTURES IN WINE COUNTRY

Linda Kaplan

The Lyons Press

Guilford, Connecticut

An imprint of The Globe Pequot Press

The Lyons Press is an imprint of The Globe Pequot Press.

10 9 8 7 6 5 4 3 2 1

Printed in the United States of America

Library of Congress Cataloging-in-Publication Data

Kaplan, Linda.
    My first crush: misadventures in wine country / Linda Kaplan.
        p. cm.
    ISBN 1-59228-610-0 (trade cloth)
        Wine and wine making—Oregon—McMinnville—Miscellanea. I. Title.

TP557.K355 2005
641.2'2'0979539—dc22

                                                                                    2005040768

PHOTOGRAPHS BY RON KAPLAN.
MAP BY DAVID PETTERSON.

Epigraph to *My First Crush* is reprinted with permission of Simon & Schuster Adult Publishing
Group from *The Sun Also Rises* by Ernest Hemingway. Copyright 1926 by Charles Scribner's
Sons. Copyright renewed 1954 by Ernest Hemingway.

Author's Note:
This story is real, though a few of the place and character names have been disguised for the
sake of privacy. To make the book more entertaining, I've included some events that happened
beyond the first year we owned Panther Creek.

In Gratitude:

Thanks to my mom, Phyllis Bittner, for inspiring me. Thanks to my longtime writing colleagues, Irene Parikhal, Megan Taylor, and Jim Dolan for keeping me on track. Thanks to my agent, Angela Rinaldi, and editor, Ann Treistman, for believing in me. Most of all, thanks to my real first crush and husband, Ron Kaplan, for taking the chance which made all of this possible.

"This wine is too good for toast-drinking, my dear.
You don't want to mix emotions up with a wine like that.
You lose the taste."

—ERNEST HEMINGWAY, *The Sun Also Rises*

CONTENTS

Premium Pinot Noir

Serves approximately 72,000
(36,000 bottles)

50 tons of the finest Pinot Noir grapes
4 kg yeast, not wild
8 kg yeast food

Rise at the crack of dawn and hand-cut perfectly ripened Pinot Noir grapes. Place the grape clusters in half-ton bins. Speed fruit by flatbed truck to the winery. (Do not allow rain to touch the grapes or the wine will be watery.)

Immediately sort every cluster by hand, discarding foreign matter, leaves, unripe fruit, and rot.

Gently crush grapes with a destemmer-crusher. Discard stems.

Transfer juice, pulp, skins, and seeds into refrigerated steel tanks or plastic fermenters. Cover.

Wait two days and add yeast. Wait two more days and sprinkle in yeast food. Cover.

Ferment. At least once a day punch down the skins, pulp, and seeds.

After fermentation press solid matter away from wine. Let wine settle in tank. Rack (move) to barrels.

Barrel wine approximately sixteen months. Test to make certain wine has passed through malolactic fermentation.

Bottle using only the highest-quality Portuguese corks. For best results, wait another five years before serving.

Note: Worry and brooding at each stage are necessary to raise the finest qualities in the wine.

*Panther Creek Cellars is located just off the main drag
in the town of McMinnville, Oregon.*

 CHAPTER 1

Isn't It Romantic?

I'M FAIRLY CERTAIN I'd never heard of McMinnville. I'd never heard of it, that is, until that pivotal August weekend when my husband signed the papers to purchase Panther Creek Cellars, lock, stock, and a few barrels. The winery crouches in mid-McMinnville, home to just over twenty thousand Oregonians. Two blocks off the town's main drag and two blocks from the county jail, the lime-stained, redbrick winery is constrained by a chain-link fence softened by invasive ivy and a stand of old roses. Railroad tracks, some structures of questionable function, and a feed store border the property.

What flight of fancy incited an Iowa construction lawyer and his foot-dragging wife—a part-time ad copywriter, part-time newspaper correspondent, and full-time mother—to think they could run a winery? The answer has nothing to do with education or experience. As I see it now, the answer lies in a rare confluence of impending empty-nest syndrome and what my husband Ron sensed was a once-in-a-lifetime opportunity. Both of us were teetering on the cusps of our fiftieth birthdays.

Snared in a flash of emotional frailty initiated by jamming dorm sheets in my daughter's undersized suitcase, I had, in theory, I suppose, agreed to this life-altering event. My concentration and emotions were confined to the imminent launch of our second child.

"Okay," I'd said to Ron, quickly weighing the odds of this latest long shot.

We'd been married for more than a quarter century; I'd seen brainstorms build on his horizons with cyclonic fury and then blow themselves out with no damage to the status quo. Ron is the kind of guy with plenty of interests beyond wine: fly fishing, bicycling, photography, and cooking. Purchasing a winery was as far-fetched as his buying a fishing lodge in Minnesota, a restaurant in Paris. So when he took off for Oregon, I never believed the winery sale would close so abruptly and our new life would begin without opportunity to hash and rehash.

"Panther Creek," he repeated long-distance, as if unable to conceive of his own good fortune. "I love that Pinot Noir." By now, the deed was all but done.

"How big is McMinnville?" I asked.

"Small, but . . ."

"Does it have a library?" I interrupted.

"Carnegie."

"Health club?"

"Women only."

"Bakery?"

"Check," he said. "Check, check, check."

Feeling suspicious, I asked to speak with our older daughter who was scouting with her dad.

"He's right; you're going to love it," she promised. I should have known right then they were in cahoots.

As their exhilaration spun through the phone lines, I glanced around, suddenly adoring our recently remodeled West Des Moines kitchen: contemporary cabinets, wood floors, and, at last, a clever hiding place for all my pots and pans. The sun splashed on my gleaming range top.

"We won't have to move there, will we?" I asked. Ron said he didn't think so, but in my heart of hearts, I felt warning palpitations. Suddenly my ears were buzzing, and the sound had nothing to do with the connection. It was the drone of high anxiety.

"The winery building's historic," he wheedled. Ron was smitten. Even Panther Creek's tired physical structure offered irresistible cachet—for him.

"How about the vineyards?" I asked, brightening a little as I imagined lush vines tumbling down rolling hillsides. Somewhere, perhaps in the paper pile near that very phone, I had a photo of Francis Ford Coppola's digs in Napa.

"It didn't come with grapevines. The winery's right in town."

Panic swelled in my throat. How in God's name could a person make wine without vineyards?

"Long-term leases," he said. "I'll explain it all when I get home."

Like it or not, we were already immersed in the wine business, purple to the elbows.

LEASED VINEYARD PROPERTY

Panther Creek is located among a grid of city streets, not in the country-side. The first myth about wineries is that they must sit on vineyard property. A winery is the place where grapes are processed, not grown.

Even in France, wineries enter into long-term contracts with grape farmers to lease particular parcels of vineyard property. Flavor diversity of the wines is one important reason for this practice. Characteristics such as flavor and nose (aroma or bouquet) result from the particular ecosystem where grapes grow. Some sites are hotter than others, some are at higher altitude, some are wetter, some are windier. Diversity creates more interesting, more complex blends and allows the single vineyard wines more distinctive personalities when compared to each other.

Panther Creek brings in grapes from several Willamette Valley vineyards, all well within a day's drive from the winery. (Picked grapes should not go more than a day without being refrigerated or they will begin to rot.)

Bednarik and Shea vineyards, two of Panther Creek's grape sources, are located about fifteen miles apart, both to the north of the winery. The fruit-flavor profiles of these wines differ dramatically. Bednarik Pinot Noir is often rich in spice and pepper; Shea is redolent of red fruit and earth. The grapes from Freedom Hill Vineyard, located about twenty miles to the south of the winery, create a third wine that is recognizably highly structured (good tannins, perceived by a dry feeling on your tongue, and acid for aging) with a black-cherry flavor. Is it the clone (the genetic makeup of the plant), the soil, the winds off the coast range, or the slope of the hillside that produces these flavors? The answer is probably all of the above.

The winemaker is at nature's mercy when all the grapes come from a single vineyard. In addition to frost, botrytis (mold), phylloxera (an insect), and hungry flocks of birds are a few common vineyard plagues. Diversification of vineyard sites cuts a winery's chances for losing an entire vintage because it's unlikely that frost or phylloxera will hit two separate vineyards at the same time.

For some time Ron had toyed, mostly in the privacy of his own mind, with the idea of owning a winery. After completing a cooking course at La Varenne in Paris, he embarked on a friendship and business venture with the owners of the school. This association involved traveling to Burgundy where he was bewitched by Pinot Noir, the finicky grape, the capricious grape, which crushed and fermented makes the most unpredictable of wines.

I quickly discovered that France's famed Côte d'Or vineyards and the northern Willamette Valley lie along similar lines of latitude. While

France's experience with Pinot Noir has persevered for centuries, the genesis of Oregon's great Pinot Noir adventure took root much, much later, in the 1960s.

Decades after that, my adventures and misadventures with wine— any wine—had yet to begin. It's true that winter after winter Ron had asked me to consider a move; we were both fed up with an annual six months of shoveling, scraping, salting, slipping, sliding, and crashing. I *had* agreed to make a break to more favorable climes *sometime* in the future.

The December before he bought the winery, Ron had skidded his car down our ski slope of a driveway; the event ended with a breath-taking spin into our daughter's parked Honda. Ron sustained a single injury, a bruised ego, with symptoms manifested in X-rated expletives each time snowflakes drifted toward the driveway. The winter before that a delivery girl, the steaming Domino's pizza box still in her hands, stood on our porch and watched as her parked car slid through our closed garage door. Oregon, offering no more than a flurry of annual snowfall and an infrequent slick of ice, was on our short list of future relocation options. But, a winery?

I replayed my husband's phone call again and again in my brain. Could we actually do business on the edge of the continent in a town where I wasn't acquainted with another human being? Have I mentioned that I didn't know Pinot Noir from Pinot Gris, Cabernet from Chardonnay?

Ron and I were born and raised in Iowa; our children were raised in Iowa. The reactions of our friends and coworkers to our purchase ranged from shock to bewilderment. Soon Ron quit working at the law firm to concentrate on winery business, replacing his leather briefcase with a floppy canvas satchel, his three-piece suits with flannel shirts and khakis. He traded the sedan, which he still begrudged for the sliding incident, for a four-wheel-drive vehicle with clearance for vineyard excursions. His ex-partners at the law firm hinted they would hold his job. Iowans, even citified Iowans, understand the nuances of corn and soybean agribusiness. Wine grapes are alien.

We know some people thought we were crazed. And maybe we were. I come from a family of accomplished worriers, not to mention teetotalers. But rising to the occasion, they slapped our backs, wished us well, and toasted our venture with sweaty glasses of iced tea.

My ninety-three-year-old Baptist grandmother, a sliver of a woman whose size belied the magnitude of her familial clout, was eager to discuss grapes and vineyards. They'd trellised table grapes in her backyard until the forties, when, she said, an overdose of field-crop herbicides annihilated every vine in the state. (By then Prohibition had already shut down Iowa's fledgling wine industry.)

While the subject of grapes was conversation fodder, wineries and fermented grapes were not; distillers and vintners, in my grandmother's mind, ranked with reckless drivers, telemarketers, and people who refuse to rake leaves from their yards. Menaces to society. Yet I watched as she strained to make an exception for her flesh and blood, me. A mention of communion wine fell on deaf ears. At last, she patted my arm and said she'd always enjoyed grape jelly. That was that.

"How big are your vineyards?" the other relatives asked trying to join in the spirit of the occasion. This question, in particular, clenched my stomach, though I tried to answer with a confident smile.

For years I'd been a correspondent at the *Des Moines Register,* where I'd started out tracking down school lunch menus and moved up to writing some of the lead stories in the features section. I'd recently completed a series on growing old in Iowa.

"There's a long shot we could move to Oregon," I told one of my editors. I thought he'd be up in arms, losing a steady stringer like me.

His protests would be gratifying even if the move didn't pan out.

"What's writing like these days?" he asked.

"Finally, it's easy. I used to spend hours on every paragraph, searching for the right words."

"Maybe your life has gotten a little too easy," he said, returning to his editing.

What? I thought we were friends. That was certainly not the response I'd hoped for. I put on my sweater and gathered my papers.

"See you next week," I grumbled.

"Life should be an adventure," he said without ever looking away from his screen. "Tell Ron I said to go for it."

Fat chance I'd be passing that along.

My women friends invited me out to lunch and offered up encouraging bits of advice. When I expressed concerns about moving to Oregon, they promised that *if* it happened, they would visit. They scribbled out the names of college friends and cousins who were located in the Portland area. They talked about the romance of winemaking—but when I asked them to be more explicit, they were as befuddled as I was. Drinking wine could be romantic, but making it? Who knew?

Initially the winery seemed unreal to me. Ron, on the other hand, hit the ground running. There were contracts to sign, barrels to buy, labels to get approved, employees to hire. I read *New! Wine for Dummies* and wished for the *Old!* version. Maybe it was more basic. Even after several trips to McMinnville, I felt completely ineffective, like a puppet with cut strings.

I quickly learned white Zinfandel is not the choice of the oenosuave, though I'd enjoyed this wine for years with everything from shrimp salad to sirloin steak. Soon after the purchase, I was certain I saw our country club wine steward—a zippy woman who reveled in wine talk with Ron—eyeing me pityingly. Now Ron struggled to introduce me to the nuances of Pinot Noir. I wasn't sure I could discern the flavors of black cherries or raspberries in the glass.

"Is it wrong to taste grapes?" I asked.

"Yes," Ron said. The wine steward flinched.

At a neighborhood gathering, a friend advised me to grasp my wine glass by the stem.

"Why?" I asked, rearranging my fingers.

"I think the wine gets too warm if you hold it at the top. Anyway, that's how they do it in the *Wine Spectator*," she said. *Wine Spectator*? Was everyone but me an expert?

The owner of a wineshop in our West Des Moines neighborhood asked if we would like to host a tasting of Panther Creek wines.

"Absolutely," Ron answered. The buzzing had started in my ears again so it's difficult to recall the rest of that conversation.

On the appointed evening a polite queue of tasters filed past our table, which was swathed in white linens at the back of the store. I smiled and kept my lips zipped. I poured with trembling hands. I dabbed at wine stains with a napkin. I smiled and poured some more. When someone asked a question, I nodded toward the shopowner or toward Ron so they would answer.

Finally, a couple I'd known since high school filed by. Seeing them while I was pouring wine gave me a curious, tender feeling—as when once on a sunny boulevard thousands of miles from home, Ron and I had serendipitously crossed paths with a neighbor.

I wasn't close friends with this couple, but we had history.

"You're brave," they said. Every time someone said we were brave, I felt more cowardly.

I watched as they rolled the Panther Creek Pinot Noir over their tongues. They nodded enthusiastically. I'd cheered for this man when he played high school basketball for our hometown team. Forty years earlier I'd earned Girl Scout merit badges with the girl who became his wife. I thought back to the two of us, schoolbooks in tow, waiting for a ride to our Red Cross first-aid class.

A jolt passed through me, acknowledging that very soon Ron and I could be deserting friends like these. It was the writing on the wall, the grapes in the bins, the wine in the bottles. It was the terrible truth. I knew it before Ron knew it. I excused myself to empty the spit bucket, something I'd recently vowed I'd never do. I needed to wipe my eyes.

Returning to the table with the empty bucket, my emotions curbed, I was again prepared to pour. Finally someone asked me directly—there was no way to put this question off on Ron—if we were going to stick with Pinot Noir or if we would consider making a Burgundy wine.

Wait a minute. I could actually answer this question. Just as suddenly as my heart had sunk, it sung. I had just read that in France wine is named after the region where it's produced. Pinot Noir, with a very few exceptions, is known as Burgundy when it's produced in that region of France, just as sparkling wine is Champagne when it hails from France's Champagne region. *Très bon,* Linda. Apparently one person in the state of Iowa knew less about wine than I did.

Wine Notes

STAGE A WINE TASTING

I attended my first wine tasting at the Des Moines wineshop after Ron and I purchased Panther Creek. Ron was familiar with wine tastings; I, of course, didn't know pips.

Since then I've learned a wine tasting involves nothing more than opinions. No taster is right in his or her likes or dislikes; no one is wrong.

Palates (each person has more than nine thousand one-of-a-kind taste buds) differ, tastes are subjective, and learning what you like to drink is the point of a wine tasting.

If you're staging a wine tasting at your home, you need a few items to stay organized. Put out some paper and pens so folks can take notes and keep track of their favorite selections. Set buckets up and down the table; most participants will want to discard the wine left in their glasses after a taste or two. I don't encourage amateurs to spit—especially in a dining room setting.

You may want some pitchers of water on the table for rinsing glasses, though this is not necessary. Put a white napkin at each place so participants can hold their glasses against the napkin to get an idea of the wine's color. Finally, cut up some French bread and have it available for people who want to cleanse their palate between tastes. The wines themselves are often left in brown paper bags so tasters won't be unduly influenced by predetermined good (or bad) vintages and vineyards.

Horizontal or vertical tastings are common because they yield the best comparisons. A horizontal tasting might involve wines produced by several wineries in a single vintage, or several wines produced by a particular winery in a single vintage: for example, Panther Creek's Shea Vineyard Pinot Noir, Panther Creek's Freedom Hill Pinot Noir, and Panther Creek's Bednarik Pinot Noir from 2004. A vertical tasting could include multiple vintages of one particular wine. Naturally the technique works for any vintner's wines, and you can find plenty of help choosing at your area wineshop. Pour only an ounce or two of wine in each person's wine glass.

Here are some questions to start the conversation.

Color

1. What is the color of the wine?
2. Does the color look saturated or thin?

Nose

3. Is there a bouquet (aroma)? What does it remind you of? First decide if

the wine emits organic or inorganic aromatics. Then, for example, if you get fruity, floral, or herbal notes, break those aromas down. Perhaps you'll find strawberries or blueberries. Honeysuckle or roses. Perhaps the wine has an earthy, mushroomy bouquet.

4. Slow down a minute and swirl your wine. Do you notice any new aromas after the wine is aerated? Do you notice any disagreeable odors?

Mouth Feel

6. What is the texture of the wine in your mouth? What writers refer to as a dense, chewy (not literally, of course) texture is often an indication of barreling time.

7. Does the wine feel slightly hot on your tongue? This may mean the wine is high in alcohol.

Palate

8. Does the flavor seem robust or delicate? Can you pick out two or three specific flavors?

9. Try moving the wine from one area of your mouth to another. What is the first flavor you get? The second? Is there a third? Inhale gently through your mouth before swallowing.

10. Swirl the glass and try again. As air mixes with the wine, the flavors may change. What foods could you successfully pair with this wine?

11. Often oak, vanilla, smoke, coconut, and butterscotch flavors are the result of barreling. Do these flavors override the others?

12. Does the wine taste sweet or dry (no residual sugar)?

13. Are the acids, tannins (puckery sensation), and fruit balanced? Do you think this wine would improve with cellaring?

14. Do you notice a long finish (flavor that lingers once you've swallowed)? Is the finish pleasant?

At the end of the tasting, it's fun to determine the group's favorite and compare its price to the others. Don't feel embarrassed if you discover you're enamored with an inexpensive wine; feel happy. Then try to discover what others find pleasing in their favorite wines.

The day after the wineshop tasting we climbed back on a plane to Portland. Despite my moment of glory at the tasting, my subconscious thoughts scuttled to the subversive. There were plenty of answers I didn't have. As soon as I stepped into the airport, I was plagued with new problems—sneezing, hacking, nose blowing, and hives. Yes, splotchy hives. The symptoms didn't abate. On each successive trip to Oregon, I itched. While Ron researched French glass and Portuguese corks, I studied up on antihistamines and homeopathic remedies, staked out pharmacies, and hung around health food stores. A pale clerk (not the picture of health) with even paler gray hair touted fish oil. She diagnosed that my entire immune system was languishing in the shock of recent events. The woman, her skinny arms flaying until her flat breasts flipped in her dress, glared at Ron.

"Three times a day," she advised, riveting her steel-gray eyes on me and tapping the bottle cap with a thorny-gray fingernail.

I downed a single swallow of the vile, milky fluid.

"My God!" I hollered, panting through my nose. No amount of water could purge the taste from my tongue, my lips, my teeth. Talk about a ruined palate.

A long history of women had faced the West with spunk and deter-mination. Not me. My response was psychosomatic, but knowing isn't curing. And miserable is miserable. I devoured Annie Dillard's book on the Pacific Northwest in the late 1800s and the settlers' struggle for survival in that mud-sucked setting. The novel was called *The Living*, and I knew I would have fallen among "the expiring."

Soon after our purchase I paid a visit to my longtime Iowa dentist. By coincidence he was a member of Ron's wine-tasting group. I had never partaken in their tastings, although I'd been a guest at some of the group's lavish dinner parties. As I lay gap-mouthed and drooling, Bob, a bachelor without a good wife to tell him when to bite his tongue, hit me with the old saw:

"How do you make a small fortune in the wine business?"

The answer—you've heard this: "Start with a large fortune." Hives rose on my arms. What large fortune?

As Bob picked at my molars, I closed my eyes and calculated how far our family's savings could be stretched. We had a daughter just beginning her freshman year in college, another in grad school. Ron and I had quit our jobs. Retirement loomed.

Bob wiped my face and reported I'd be needing three gold crowns.

10/9 Arcus 68° Starting to kick in. Cap has formed and should see some real action soon.

10/10 ARCUS 76° P/DOWN

10/11 SUPERFOOD A3, A4 SHEA W/BLOCK
2960 gms
C3, C4 BEDNARIK C3-2200gm
C4-2400gm

10/12 HYDRO READING ARCUS TEMP 60° (SAMP) BRIX 2°
P/DOWN TEMP 79°

10/12 Received 286.5 lbs Arcus 828, Melange Block ?
1.47 tons PN 114 from Arch Summit Vyd, all in FY B's
Add 90 ml color pro; 10% whole cluster

10/12 Received 18 boxes of FH Lyre + 2 boxes Pommard
B @ 9.099 T, and 2 boxes Pommard
@ 1.011 T.   tank C
> 18 boxes Lyre into C2 - uz. 92gm 1.85 l
added 2 ... this   H₂O
— Lyre is @ 22° brix - No ????
                      added 1
> Received 8 2 boxes FH P C 10 boxes
total = WFBB/blocks) 4.791 tons total
added 50g u.2. in 1.0 l H₂O
> fruit crushed into 2B

	A	B	C		
1	56°			⊕ 525	○ = Refm on
2	56°	68°			
3		56°			
4		59°			

A page from the cellar book.

 CHAPTER 2

Where's the Recipe?

RON AND I SLIPPED INTO the winery as our unflappable interim manager Dale drizzled Pinot Noir from various bottles into several dozen balloon-shaped goblets placed on the oblong oak table. Dale spaced the glasses meticulously and answered questions in measured responses, often wordlessly: first a shrug, then a lift of the eyebrow. It was a Saturday in very late summer and my first trip to Panther Creek, just weeks after we'd signed the purchase contract. Ron and I were still living in West Des Moines, and I was still searching for the miracle that would allow us to commute between a home in Iowa and a job in Oregon. I'd been thinking the adventure of owning a winery might be okay for Ron; I was too set in my ways for an adventure (aka trauma) like moving to McMinnville.

Thick, yellow slabs of sunlight shone through the winery's long, multipaned windows and across the tasters, a group of Portland doctors. The comforting smells of fermenting fruit and yeast clung to the rows of French oak barrels. Seemingly unaware of our presence, the men turned their glasses to the light and then swirled and inhaled the vapors.

The doctors looked casual in T-shirts and jeans, yet this was serious stuff—and my first look at the marketing side of the winery. I felt a curious blend of fascination and tension. My life had swerved onto what seemed an arbitrary detour along the freeway of life, and I didn't know what to expect, outside of a colossal pileup, from one moment to the next. I just hoped none of the tasters would ask me a question.

At last the men swallowed, and their obvious delight at the sensation in their mouths allowed Ron and me, the new owners, to draw a short sigh of relief. It was then that I had a chance to look around.

I'd seen European and California wineries nudged into hillsides that had collected architectural accolades—either because of the structures' overall elegance or for their fastidious gravity flow systems (what I guessed was a favored means of moving wine). Natural stone, cool caves, exotic woods, vineyard panoramas, and a vibrant perennial garden seemed the benchmarks of these projects.

Panther Creek could have taken the booby prize. The floor plan was on a single level, nullifying what I saw as any hope of letting gravity work for us. As far as architectural features went, the front door stuck and screeched, metal against metal. Several panels had been punched out of the garage doors at the back of the building in what seemed a failed burglary. Light, air, and who knows what else streamed in the openings. The thirty-foot brick walls were veiled in molting lime. Large cracks traced the cement floors. The toilet demanded respectable intervals between flushings, never as much as twice within a half-hour. I'd been warned by Dale in his matter-of-fact way that the ancient fixture protested with foul backups when overworked.

While the building was air-conditioned, there was no furnace— and consequently, no heat. Someone at the neighborhood Circle K quick mart told me the previous owner had made wine in gloves with cut-out fingertips. It seemed everyone in McMinnville harbored shards of information about Panther Creek.

The table where the doctors gathered on that August afternoon was presentable, but the chairs had seen better days (probably in the 1950s). Each rocked on uneven legs; some were devoid of their backrests. They were mismatched—a mix of metal and plastic, some wood—but all were humbled by age and water. Though the tasting group seemed nonchalant about the setup, I elbowed Ron—Was he seeing this?—and scribbled *chairs* on my shopping list. I winced at the nonprofessional look of the cinder-block bookcases in the office. Sadly, we couldn't afford to refurnish for the sake of aesthetics.

If I squinted my eyes, I had to concede the place offered a covert charm. Perhaps it was the grand arched windows that framed the entry, the gargantuan old-growth fir beams supporting the ceiling, or the rows of fragrant French oak barrels. Yet no dimension of charm could erase the walloping amount of work begging to be completed on the building itself.

Suddenly the whole tasting scene made me queasy. The idea of us making wine that would earn accolades by an experienced group of enthusiasts like the doctors seemed impossible. Where would we begin?

I waved Ron out of the room so I could speak to him privately.

"Did you get a recipe for the Pinot Noir?" I asked, remembering he'd said Pinot Noir would be at least ninety percent of our production. The winery had forged a reputation for a complex, ageable wine, and we planned to continue on that course.

My longtime pal Gwen had a famous recipe for brownies and I knew that I, too, had an outstanding recipe—but our results couldn't have been more different. While Gwen's brownies were gooey, mine were cakelike. A recipe for Panther Creek's bold Pinot Noir had to be stashed somewhere: the cinderblock bookcase, the closet?

Ron just stared at me.

"I mean it," I said. How would we know how to make wine without a recipe?

"There is *no* recipe," Ron whispered through clenched teeth. He looked as uptight as I felt. I knew what his exasperated expression meant. Back off with the worries. Back off with the allergies. Back off with the questions.

Frustrated, I recall the office revolving several times. I saw thousand-dollar bills slithering down winery drains.

Soon I would discover what Ron already knew. The news wasn't heartening. Even if a winemaker had a recipe for Pinot Noir, the instructions would prove useless from one vintage to the next. A person can't trust grapes and wild yeasts like she trusts flour and eggs. Even good winemakers can't clone a wine from a particularly superior vintage, though they can create a wine in a characteristic style.

Why couldn't we produce a more trustworthy wine? Other grapes, such as Sangiovese, which are the primary component of Italy's famous Chianti wines, are more fail-safe compared to Pinot Noir grapes. On a trip to sun-bronzed Tuscany, Ron and I heard again and again about the recipe for Chianti Classico. The Chianti "recipe," or formula, is literally spelled out in Italian law.

I asked a Chianti winemaker, a congenial fellow whom we'd found pruning in his vineyard, what would happen if he didn't follow the formula. A pained look flashed across the old vintner's face and, suddenly silent, he raised his crossed wrists in front of his wide leather belt.

"What's that mean?" I asked our interpreter.

"Handcuffs," she said. "He'd go to jail."

The interpreter explained that additions and omissions to the Chianti Classico recipe are truly punishable by imprisonment. The fruit must come from specific vineyards between Florence and Siena; the blend, which has changed through the decades, must include at least seventy-five percent Sangiovese grapes. Other designated grapes may be added within the proportion; acidity, aging, and alcohol percentages have to be followed to the letter. Even with these rigid requirements, each winery produces a unique product, every vintage a distinguishable wine. A written formula makes little or no difference, even in Chianti, except to enforce basic quality standards.

In the end, the quality of the grapes and the competence of the winemaker tell the tale. Experience, not a recipe, is mandatory for creating first-class Pinot Noir in Oregon, though quality grapes are also a necessity.

We had confidence in Mark Vlossak, who signed on as our winemaker the same weekend Ron purchased Panther Creek. Mark had gained years of training and experience at St. Innocent Winery, and it's a common practice for a winemaker to oversee two wineries. Without the right winemaker, there was no chance of producing a stylistically consistent wine. Ron believed that Mark could produce big, full-bodied Pinot Noirs. After a long meeting at that famous breakfast bistro, the International House of Pancakes, the men struck a deal. Mark would determine what equipment was needed and get it ordered and installed before harvest, which was only a few weeks away. In the end Mark agreed to outfit the winery and act as winemaker at least through the first year. No one argued the man had his work cut out for him.

I liked the fact that Mark was also a licensed physician's assistant. Having ruled out fish oil, I hoped he'd have some tips about my allergies. Additionally, the winery was replete with opportunities for catastrophe. Wet floors, tanks of pressurized gases, and towers of glass bottles—to name a few.

The new Rauch destemmer-crusher arrived looking like a stainless steel casket with a mortifying don't-do-this picture plastered on its side. (This is the machine that crushes grapes and spits the stems into a pile on the floor.) The unwary winery worker in the drawing on the destemmer-crusher had stuck his entire body—Could that be accidental?—in the machine and come out braided. I would have guessed shredded, but those German engineers know their products.

In addition to the destemmer-crusher, we replaced the outdated equipment we'd inherited with nine refrigerated custom-made tanks, a refrigeration system with piping for thirteen tanks, a must (the mash of seeds, skins, pulp, and juice) pump, a wine-transfer pump, dozens of barrels, and giant racks to get the barrels off the floor and into the vertical spaces—of which the winery had a surplus.

Even as the first bins of grapes (we tested the machinery and ourselves with some run-throughs) were dropped off at the winery, Mark was called from the vineyards to wire the motor on a winch that raised the lid on a refrigerated tank. Ron was on the phone trying to track a tank that had been lost on Interstate 5 somewhere between Santa Rosa,

California, and McMinnville. We found it difficult to believe someone could misplace a shiny, stainless steel, 2,300-gallon tank spacious enough to hold approximately nine hundred cases of wine, though there's an axiom in the universe that things get lost in a direct relationship to how desperately they're needed.

Meanwhile Dale, the interim manager, was trying to teach me the basics of winemaking. This proves he's unflappable. I squeaked along beside him—wearing my new rubber overalls, elbow-length gloves, and boots—tasting the grapes, peering into bins, feeling the heat of fermentation, then smelling the must as it evolved to wine.

Early in that first vintage, before I was enlightened, I took notes— determined to scribble out a recipe for Panther Creek's signature Pinot Noir. If you follow my recipe precisely from one year to another (you'll find it in the preface of this book), results will, alas, *never* be predictable—mostly because of the frustratingly fickle Pinot Noir grape. What's lacking, making this recipe bogus, is the secret ingredient, an element that cannot be recorded. It's the winemaker's magic. Bin by bin and barrel by barrel the winemaker tastes and tweaks. Mark, like all good winemakers, added a certain amount of brooding to his mix, which roused mysterious qualities in the wine.

We have a neighbor who makes wine in his basement, and, I guarantee, he doesn't go through all these gyrations. Without any intervention whatsoever, wine will actually make itself. Winemaking is like childbirth. It can be easy—or not.

Making a simple wine in small quantities is an attainable goal. Fill a bucket with grapes, leave it in a warm spot, and within a couple weeks you can filter off the thick stuff and, *voilà!*, drink the wine. After tasting your creation, you'll probably wish you'd intervened during fermentation with options such as yeasts, yeast foods (sometimes the little guys demand a particular diet), or cooling.

Fine winemaking requires the winemaker's control—or at the very least, a close monitor of the process. Mother Nature takes the lead, but the winemaker shows her the way.

Wine Notes

THE CELLAR BOOK

Each year the winemaker, lab assistant, and cellarmaster record the steps from bin to bottle in a cellar book. The information includes specifics from smells emitted from the must during fermentation to the names of the coopers who made the barrels where the wine aged.

Vague recollections aren't good enough for the Bureau of Alcohol, Tobacco and Firearms agents who want to know how many tons of grapes the winery received on what date. (They want to know this to determine if the number of bottles produced jibes with the amount of grapes brought into the winery, since alcohol is taxed.)

For winemaking purposes, notes are used for reflection on the particular harvest—not to replicate it. At best, winemaking is an alchemy of perfectly ripened grapes, experienced judgment calls, cooperative weather, exhausting work completed in good time, and, as I said, a bit of magic.

Cleaning the winery, and equipment like the destemmer-crusher (shown above), is a large part of harvest.

 CHAPTER 3

On the Line

D EAD CALM HUNG IN the winery. We'd had some practice runs
with the machinery, but the real work of our first harvest—aka
crush—was ahead. We attended to our jobs with guarded anxiety,
knowing that an avalanche of grapes approached. It would be crush or
be crushed.

That first harvest our crew was skeletal. Dale West, who was experienced in all aspects of the winery business, had made his services
available during the transition. Michael Stevenson, who started out as
our cellarmaster, had arrived in the West, fresh from the University of
North Carolina and brimming with Southern charm and all-American
potential. Mark Vlossak, who was born to make wine, and Jack Rovics,
a dedicated winery volunteer and bachelor cattle rancher when we met
him, hadn't been acquainted back in Wisconsin, where they were both
raised. A few other part-timers came and went that first harvest.

Mark, the winemaker, darted from vineyard to vineyard during the
days immediately preceding crush. We bit our nails while he looked,
tasted, felt, and probed for precisely ripened grapes. Mark said he
never pays much attention to the degrees brix, a scale that establishes
grape-sugar (sweetness) levels, divulged on his refractometer. When
the grapes become luscious, he asks the vineyard manager to pick. Of

course, Mark has a winemaker's palate and can discern luscious from delicious or succulent—telling, but not technical, terms. The best fruit is a balance of sugars, flavors, tannins, and acids.

Ron immediately subscribed to several weather services that he scrutinized for hourly updates. The only predictable part of weather forecasts is that each will issue a vastly different report. The first year, we were spooked by the long-term outlooks—though the weather turned into some of the best in Oregon vintage history. We learned with one-hundred-percent accuracy that forecasters warn the worst: rain blowing in from the Pacific, storms inching up from California, or sleet lashing back from the Cascades. Any one of these drippy scenarios could destroy hanging grapes. We wanted our expensive fruit safely picked and in the winery before a weather incident could occur.

All of us had our ears tuned for the sound of trucks pulling into the lot. Questions lingered. Why was the refrigeration system gurgling like an impending digestive upset? Where should we place the destemmer-crusher to avoid burning out the persnickety pump? What trucking company was delivering that stray tank from California?

We needed Mark everywhere—in the winery, as well as in the vineyards. Only the telephone broke the silence. The callers were frustrated vineyard owners and managers weathering their own storm fronts. It's always something different. Perhaps pickers showed up late; perhaps several wineries asked their grapes to be delivered on the same day; perhaps the grapes ripened unevenly and the picking was challenging. God forbid if the forecasters were right and it started to sprinkle. Mildew won't do.

SORTING IT OUT

Sorters search for sunburned and rotted grapes and throw them in bins, which are taken to the compost heap. In addition to bad fruit and foreign matter such as twisties (like the ties that close bread wrappers) and grape leaves, we also discard unripe fruit, called second crop. If the light shines just so on the sorting table, the translucent magenta color of the Pinot Noir grapes indicates unripe fruit; we obviously can't taste every cluster. When we work in poorer light at night, small size and hardness to the touch are the first clues to immaturity.

Despite the sunny summer that first year, very few grapes arrived with the small blighted areas—sickly gray in color—caused by sunburn. Some grape growers surmise that solar flares occurring during the growing season cause this condition. Sunburn is a scourge for grapes and for sorters. The sunburned sections of the clusters never ripen, so the bad grapes have to be pulled out by hand. In most cases, the good part of the cluster can be salvaged.

Rot is a tremendous problem in warm, wet vintages. Rotted clusters should be culled in the vineyard, but pickers can't catch everything, especially in a downpour. Warm, rainy harvests are rot harvests, which is why Oregon wineries queue up with the vineyard owners to pick grapes before the autumn downpours begin. Rotted clusters can be so obvious that they look like gray mice trotting along the conveyor belt—or the bad clusters can be much more covert. Spoilage is sometimes apparent only when the sorter separates the cluster for a look because that sinister rot begins on the inside.

> Occasionally, we've learned, botrytis—the fungus that rots grapes—is a good thing in white fruit. In small amounts, botrytis actually adds to the flavor of our Melon. (This wine is also known in France, where it grows in the Loire Valley, as Muscadet, and as Melon de Bourgogne in Burgundy.) The problem with rot in the vineyard, or in a bin, is that a little multiplies quickly. It's like your mother warned you: just a few bad clusters can ruin all the good grapes in no time.

The farmers try to estimate the number of tons per acre while the fruit is still hanging in the field; this allows the winery to plan how many fermentation tanks and barrels to prepare.

Imagine a vineyard situation or a trucking problem—and it happens. Once, for example, a fully loaded truck was sucked up to its wheel wells on a muddy hillside. All of these contingencies delayed the grapes' arrival at the winery. The clock's hands crawled: three, four, five, six o'clock. Everyone knew that when the grapes arrived late in the day, a long night of processing that fruit at the winery would follow. We yawned just thinking about the wee hours we'd see that first year.

When the first truck finally rolled through the winery gate, we rushed outside to watch an event that, within a day or so, became so pedestrian we wouldn't bother to raise our tired eyes. Michael Stevenson roared around on the forklift unloading bins from the truck and stacked them on the tarmac behind the winery.

Once all the fruit was off a truck, Michael forklifted a bin at a time into the dumper. From the dumper, the grapes tumbled onto a conveyor where the fast-fingered sorters stood.

Wine grapes look slightly different than table grapes. Pinot Noir grows in small, tight, purple clusters, while table grapes are larger with the berries spaced more loosely in their clusters. Individually, Pinot Noir grapes resemble blueberries—but it's impossible to separate a single berry without crushing the rest. Taste Pinot Noir as you would sample a plum or an apple, by biting into the cluster. Even at the sorting table, flavor is the crucial test of ripeness. I tasted that first crush until canker sores disabled my tongue.

In most cases, sorting is the process that distinguishes premium from middling Pinot Noirs. At one time or another during crush, everyone in the winery sorts. Occasionally when the grapes are of optimal ripeness and the berries so primo, sorting can be a waste. In those rare instances, the sorters' time can be better spent elsewhere—even if that means some well-earned loafing.

That first year we sorters toiled with makeshift equipment. The scene looked like this: Michael dumped half-ton bins of grapes into the dumper with the forklift. (The dumper was situated about four feet above one end of the conveyor belt.) The sorters stood along the moving belt, which trundled grapes from where they fell from the dumper to the destemmer-crusher. We tipped that dumper a billion times—or maybe it just seemed like a billion times.

None of us guessed that some other wineries were using shaker tables. With a shaker table the grapes are joggled into a single layer before the fruit gets to the conveyor belt. I remember the anxiety of trying to cull a few clusters of rot from mounds of grapes and still keep pace with the fruit that was passing in front of me.

"Grab that cluster," a partner on the other side of the conveyor belt would exclaim.

I'd glance around wildly. "Which one? Which one? Where?"

In addition, we balanced on the heavy pipes that supported the table, instead of standing on the floor. Added height allowed us to bend over rather than reach up to the fruit. My rubber boots, and my feet inside, sort of curled around the pipes as I balanced, grasping a vertical support with my free hand. I don't know which ached more at night, my feet or my back. I'm embarrassed to say how long I waited before purchasing step stools; their fixed, flat foundations felt as if we were sorting from easy chairs compared to the rolled-foot torture of the pipes.

The person in charge of the mechanism that controlled the jerry-built dumper performed a delicate task. When too many grapes fell, sorting became impossible. The sorters were occasionally buried and forced to stop the conveyor and regroup. We then pushed the avalanche of grapes in front of us apart with our forearms. The full-forearm sweep, utilized to separate the mound of grapes, is both sticky and backbreaking. And it's ticklish when you consider the possibility of a buried yellow jacket.

"What kind of job is this?" I demanded of Ron more than once that first year. My hands were sticky, my clothes were sticky, my hair was sticky. At times the soles of my boots felt pasted to the floor.

"Don't sort if you don't like it," he'd say.

Who would *like it?* The alternative was staying at home or in our room at the B&B while all the action was at the winery. When I stayed behind, I wondered how the grapes looked, where the guys ate lunch, what they were talking about. Soon I was back on the line.

Sorters discard all foreign material that arrives with the grapes. I've never figured out how metal twisties get into the grapes, but occasionally they do. If twisties snuck past us, they'd play havoc with the machinery. Fortunately, foreign objects could never land in a bottle of wine because of a coarse filter, dubbed a *bugcatcher*, through which all wine must pass on its way to the bottle.

"Don't let the pump run dry," Mark would yelp as the conveyor belt backed up with grapes. This happened when our new destemmer-crusher clogged with grape skins and stems. The pump that moves must (the combination of juice and solids) between the destemmer-crusher and the tanks looks something like a vacuum cleaner with several switches and two hoses. Liquid goes in one hose and through the pump, then comes out another hose. The pump's purpose is to gently push the must, or other liquids, between containers. Apparently a pump that runs dry destroys the motor.

Whenever Mark raised the alarm seven of us bolted from the conveyor and ran toward our costly new pump. But Mark was the only one who actually knew how to shut it down. So we wrung our hands and groped for an emergency shut-down button, lever, switch—Wouldn't it be red?—certain the machine was already sucking air until Mark could extricate himself from some other job to cut the power.

Several times that first harvest my unique talents were called upon to root out dry clogs in the pump hoses: I was the only one with hands small enough to circumvent its internal channels.

Between running dry and clogging, the pump was the nemesis of the vintage. Yet on one memorable night, our complication involved the motor on the dumper.

We met Melody, as I recall, just before midnight. We'd already been sorting for hours. Melody had worked the evening shift at the lumberyard, which was her regular job. She had somehow been cajoled by Jack—Panther Creek's indispensable volunteer, a regular shopper at Melody's place of employment, and obviously a smooth talker—into spending the rest of the night helping out at Panther Creek. Melody is not your typical blonde. She's too pretty to be the girl next door, too wholesome-looking to be part of the Hollywood scene. But could she work? That was my unspoken question when we met that night, sealing our bond beside the conveyor belt with a sticky handshake. I became less confident of Melody's capabilities when I had to remind her to tie up those flaxen locks lest they snag in the moving conveyor.

In spite of the fact that each of us had worked all day, it was Melody—younger, I rationalized—who jumped down off her stool and hosed out the used bins between sorting jobs so Michael could forklift the containers out of our way. I was first impressed by Melody's energy and later by her mastery of the hose.

A garter snake is to a boa constrictor as a garden hose is to a winery hose. The winery hose is equipped with a very tricky trigger sprayer. Despite an obvious arrow, the spray nozzle seems to be attached backwards on the hose. The unwary water jockey who fails to heed the arrow all but knocks him or herself backwards with the torrent of icy-cold water that explodes from the nozzle. Everybody at the winery has taken a beating from the trigger sprayer—except, I noted from the corner of my eye, Melody.

The clock hands were creeping toward the 2:00 A.M. mark when a grinding sound erupted from the motor that powers the dumper mechanism that drops the grapes on the conveyor. Everything screeched to a halt; we had dozens of full half-ton bins outside on the tarmac still needing to be sorted. Melody and I rinsed the purple off our hands and arms and twiddled our thumbs while the guys tore into the defunct motor and, in desperation, cannibalized other equipment, including light switches, for working parts. If they're not processed, picked grapes rot quickly. Ron would have disassembled his new Land Cruiser if he thought it would have helped. Precious minutes passed. I felt the dregs of energy oozing out of me. Even talking was exhausting.

"If you'll sort, I could use the forklift to dump the grapes directly on the conveyor," Melody suggested.

That woke me up. The thought of Melody at the forklift controls seemed hilarious in my diminished state. I could only imagine her crashing through the tanks, ramming the bins, crushing the crusher.

All I said was, "Let's wait for Michael."

"I'm certified," she interrupted. "At least we'd be doing something."

"Certified?"

"A certified forklift operator."

"Go for it," I said.

The minute Melody swung onto the forklift, Michael was at her side. "What's going on?" he asked, twisting some colored electrical wires in his hands. The new forklift was Michael's baby.

"She's certified," I said. Our eyes froze on Melody as she delicately balanced a bin on the forks, lifted, and tilted ever so slightly, then trickled the grapes onto the moving conveyor. About an hour later when the motor was humming again, Melody and I were several bins ahead of the game.

The conveyor belt travels more slowly when the grapes are problematic, allowing more time for conversation. Sorting is boring; talk is salvation. From the start I learned Oregonians are intriguing storytellers, which, I believe, stems from the fact that most people have migrated from other places and are stories themselves. I no longer marvel at the saga of a New York stockbroker who chucked a six-figure salary to raise goats in the Willamette Valley, or an airplane pilot who turned in his flight plans to grow herbs and mesclun. The more I learned about Yamhill County, the less I felt like an outsider. I begged to hear all the tales—tall and true.

Once the storytelling began, entire histories spilled out. I've heard tales from fourth-generation Oregonians about ancestors forced to discard hand-carved bed frames, precious family heirlooms, and wedding gowns to lighten loads for their oxen as they scaled the Cascades, sometimes within sight of their destinations. I've heard about a gypsy curse and a series of mysterious fires in the 1860s that resulted in a midnight relocation of the Yamhill County seat from the city of Lafayette to the city of McMinnville, a distance of about five miles. Now I look at the empty streets of Lafayette, once teeming with riverboat travelers, and wonder what might have been.

"Is there really a Panther Creek?" I asked, using my forearm to spread the clusters more evenly across the conveyor belt.

"North of town," was the answer. The creek runs along Panther Creek Road. Before long Ron and I went exploring, searching out the timber-shaded byway. Mule deer played on its shoulders. Turkey hawks circled, waiting—I supposed—for one of the deer to saunter a little too close to oncoming traffic. Drivers take these backroad corridors at disconcertingly high speeds. Oregon roads aren't laid out in simple one-mile grids like they are in the flatlands. Oregon roads circumvent too many hills and mountains to run directly from point A to point B.

I learned, probably on the conveyor belt, that the early Oregon settlers had called cougars "panthers." A new acquaintance told me she'd spotted two of the big yellow cats carousing on her hillside property outside McMinnville—as if they owned the place. In fact, they did; my friend was forced to give up her after-dinner walks. Cougars have been known to stalk humans. They devour pets like hors d'oeuvres.

After about eight hours on the line we ran out of stories and small talk, leaving ample time to complain about bee stings, earwigs, hunger pangs, caffeine withdrawal, stained fingernails, headaches, sun in the eyes, swollen ankles, and aching backs. Without the right mindset, sorting seems endless.

It was Jack, a man who doesn't complain, who advised me to seek the Zen in grape sorting. When he first mentioned it, I thought Zen, a fresh interpretation of reality, could serve as the ultimate antidote for our pain. Jack would be the master; the other sorters would be his disciples. While we hunkered down on the line, Jack would unleash the secrets of life.

I threw out my first question gleaned from scraps of information— or, as it turned out, misinformation—I'd probably gathered back in my college years.

"Why would a sorter want to become one with the grapes?" (Within seconds of passing beneath our hands, the fruit is mangled in the destemmer-crusher.)

Jack and Ben, a part-timer who had once considered the Roman Catholic priesthood, hastily pointed out that Zen is self-taught through experience, not talking.

Great. If I'd experienced Zen, I wouldn't have asked for an explanation. From what I gathered, however, one of the tenets of this ancient understanding is the importance of living in the moment. For example, it didn't behoove me to begin obsessing by midafternoon that I'd probably still be sorting grapes well into the midnight hours. I gave it a try and began to take Jack's advice to go with the flow of an unperceiving conveyor. Perhaps, for me, that was a new level of insight. And once going with the flow, I also yielded to the laughter and heartfelt debates that inevitably spill out when humans stand shoulder to shoulder for hours on end.

On the other hand, I will never be able to Zen-out the earwigs. These demon insects sport oversized pincers that they use with abandon. Apparently tantalized by my pheromones, they hitch rides from the vineyards, seeking—you guessed it—me. My coworkers puzzle over how these pests venture from the bins to my person. No one ever sees. Do they crawl or fly? Has spontaneous generation actually been ruled out?

"Up your left sleeve," my coworkers advise. Every few minutes their eyes roam from the shaker table to my sweatshirt as they make their visual inspections. It's worse at night: insects are lured to our light.

"Heading for your throat," another sorter warns.

I slap futilely until some kind soul picks the earwig off my neckband and we can get back to work.

Twenty or thirty of the critters hang onto my clothes at any given time. Anyone else on the line might have one or two earwigs crawling on them. I don't feel their creepy feet or their revolting pincers, until the evil ones have lodged on my neck, my cheek, or in my hair. (Given the chance, they'll slither into your ears—hence the ghastly name.) Then I slap with sticky hands and the problem doubles and redoubles. During harvest, even after a shower, even after two showers, I invariably discover earwigs between the bedsheets with Ron and me. It's true, they've threatened our marriage.

The winegrower, Dick Shea, holds a perfect bunch of Pinot Noir.

 CHAPTER 4

Coming to Terms

VEN BEFORE THE FIRST harvest I'd been warned by our new friends in the Oregon wine business—not to mention the plumber, the clerk at the Circle K, and a woman at the beauty shop with a head full of plastic rollers—that Ron and I needed a place where we could come and go at all hours of the day and night. We needed our own appliances so we could wash our sugar-starched jeans before they dried stiff. On the occasions we finished sorting grapes at three or four in the morning, we needed a place where we could sleep until noon.

Ron and I surmised that the friendly owners of Steiger Haus Bed and Breakfast were empathetic about the trials of winemaking and willing to bend over backwards with our late hours and sticky duds—but we also guessed that breakfast after the noon hour wasn't part of their business plan.

One afternoon in early October I loafed in the sun on a lawn chair behind the winery in McMinnville. My efforts were on hold as our hanging grapes continued purpling up in the hillside vineyards outside of town. The grapes ripen at different speeds in the various vineyards. Mark was driving to and fro checking on the maturity levels of the fruit in various areas of wine country.

SWEET AND HOT

The degrees brix is an interesting figure that reflects grape-sugar levels, showing the winemaker the chemical ripeness of grapes. A figure is attained by squeezing grape juice on the glass in a refractometer; our portable refractometer is about the size of a flashlight. The degrees brix indicate to what degree the grape juice bends light, which relates to the amount of sugar in the juice. Higher sugars mean riper grapes.

Winemakers in the Willamette Valley look for a reading in the vicinity of twenty-two to twenty-four degrees brix for Pinot Noir. Other varietals have slightly different targets. This procedure is often performed with the grape farmer so a picking decision can be made.

During fermentation sugar becomes alcohol; when a wine is completely dry (a term meaning not sweet), all of the sugar in the grapes has been converted. With a refractometer to measure sugar levels, a winemaker can determine a wine's final percentage of alcohol even before the grapes are picked.

You don't need to be a math wizard to figure this out. Approximately half the grapes' degrees brix translates to the alcohol level of a dry wine. Because sugar levels generally rise the longer the grapes hang on the vine, a winemaker who picks the grapes early will produce a low-alcohol wine; if he picks late, he'll make a high-alcohol wine.

Picking decisions depend on factors other than a refractometer reading. The Willamette Valley's cool nights let the grapes reach ripeness slowly. Slow ripening allows the flavors to peak at the same time the grapes become ripe. Slow ripening presents an opportunity for the most complex, interesting, and luxuriant flavors to develop in Pinot Noir. Remember that Pinot Noir is a finicky grape that needs to be finessed even on the vines. If a climate (or a particular autumn) is too hot, Pinot Noir reaches ripeness and can begin to rot before flavors can fully develop.

If it's a hot harvest and the wine becomes too alcoholic, some wineries add water to their wine to achieve lower alcohol levels. In years when rain begins before the sugars rise high enough, some wineries add sugar to the juice to raise the final alcohol content. The best scenario is to pick perfectly ripened grapes so one does not have to resort to these interventions.

Near the winery yellow leaves on the treetops flirted with the azure sky. The scent of the early fruit we'd processed in test runs had attracted a steady swarm of bees to the crush pad. They buzzed about their business as I lounged, more asleep than awake. Ron returned from a run to the bank with a handful of roses he'd clipped from in front of the winery. Red, pink, white, and coral: a remarkable bounty for so late in the season. I took the bouquet and inhaled its sweetness.

"We have to move here, don't we?" I said at last. My heart slipped into my rubber boots as I waited for his answer. I'd seen the receipts for the destemmer-crusher, the stainless steel fermenters, the American Express travel. And who could have guessed grapes would be so expensive? There was no way we could afford two residences. At this rate we could scarcely afford one. The West Des Moines house was difficult to rationalize since neither of us had a job there. Even travel between Iowa and Oregon was a chore.

I was dragging my feet because I wasn't sure I could extricate myself from my old life and friends without major adjustment problems. So much had changed in just a few weeks' time. Would I ever fit in in McMinnville? Could I become enamored with winemaking? Thus far, I wasn't captivated with the fundamentals—which hadn't, I gathered, changed in the past millennium.

Ron hesitated. "I heard about a California outfit that might be interested in buying Panther Creek," he said. "The law firm . . ." We were both tired. I could see dark circles under Ron's eyes, but I knew he didn't want to return to our old life.

I thought for a few minutes, touching the petals toughened by the nippy fall nights; they weren't as delicate as they looked from a distance.

I was just beginning to grasp the depth of Ron's fervor.

We met when I was just sixteen. Because I'm the oldest of five siblings, my younger brother and sister can't recall life without Ron. Ron driving the boat at the lake, Ron snapping photos at the family reunion, Ron fretting over a long succession of holiday beef tenderloins. By osmosis through the decades, I guess, he'd become ours and we'd become his.

When Ron is out late, I invariably rouse from sleep, often pulling from a dream, five minutes before his car turns onto our street. I listen as he closes the garage door, then creeps up the stairs and into the darkened bedroom.

Always surprised to see me turn toward the door, he says, "Did I wake you?"

"No; well, in a way," I reply.

Yet I don't read minds; I still found it unnerving I hadn't known of his yearning to own a winery until it was all but reality. Despite the jolt to our status quo, I didn't have the strength to shoulder his shattered dream.

And what about me, most ask.

I'd just begun a new chapter in my life. How could I slam the book closed before learning the whole story? Was this an adventure or a disaster?

"Let's stay," I said. My pulse was pounding so hard I could feel the reverberation in my throat. I'd weighed the pros and cons and was finally making the commitment. We agreed to put our West Des Moines home on the market after Christmas and move to McMinnville in early spring. Until then, we'd continue to fly back and forth between Iowa, where we owned the house, and Oregon, where we owned the winery.

Too edgy to continue lolling, I folded my lawn chair and went inside to place a phone order to Eddie Bauer for more jeans. I'd be needing them. I gave the catalog operator my credit card number and the winery address.

"McMinn-y-ville?" she chortled into the receiver. "Where's that?"

Men hoe Shea Vineyard's Willakenzie soil.

 CHAPTER 5

A House Is Not a Home

WHENEVER WE COULD steal away from the winery, Ron and I searched for a house in "McMinn-y-ville." I lean toward old homes. Colonial. Tudor. Saltbox. Ginger, our peppy part-time real-estate agent and a woman with a fancy for fine Pinots, thought we shouldn't overlook the convenience of new homes. Ron just wanted a house with a decent shower and a place to set the bed so he could return to his new *amour,* Panther Creek.

One early fall day while a posse of expensive plumbers tested the coolant in Panther Creek's lukewarm refrigeration system, Ron and I had little to do but drive around and worry—worry being a major component of wine—while perusing the area's real-estate market. McMinnville offered very few Tudor homes—and none for sale. The same was true for saltboxes and Colonials, large and small. Unruffled, Ginger assured us something wonderful would come on the market. Ron and I were feeling ruffled. Several house-hunting outings had already ended in failure; we weren't even tempted to make an offer.

That autumn we had circulated in the clouds between West Des Moines, Portland, Seattle (older daughter), and Boston (younger daughter). We'd sort grapes for a week or so, return to West Des Moines, and then fly back to McMinnville to sort some more. I was feeling sadness at leaving my old life; sporadically, however, the thought of starting over jolted me with excitement. Some days I was hanging on for dear life, while the following day I was ready to let go and expose myself to the great unknown. Perhaps my ex-editor had been on to something.

Ron and I were in limbo both at home and at work. Because of our irregular travel schedule, I had stopped taking writing jobs. Ron was tying up loose ends at the law firm. Technically, we owned the winery, but other people were doing most of the work. To put it mildly, we felt displaced. In addition, my daily antihistamine routine made me feel as if I were walking through life with a pillowcase over my head.

We had just lugged our suitcases into the West Des Moines house and dropped them when the phone rang. Usually it was one of the guys from the winery, but this time Ginger was on the line. She'd found the house, and it was a house in the country. This was fabulous news; the rolling hills outside McMinnville remind me of vistas I encountered as a child when I rode with Hopalong Cassidy and Roy Rogers in TV Land. Okay, they rode; I watched in my pj's.

Photographs of the grounds (*Had Ginger said grounds?*) were already in the mail. My mind turned to visions of some of the layouts I'd seen in Napa, estates I'd passed in the French countryside. The house Ginger was touting wasn't actually in a vineyard, but it overlooked a cherry or-chard. If it couldn't be grapes, cherries would do nicely.

When they arrived, the over-nighted photographs depicted a well-kept tennis court, manicured gardens, wide green lawns shaded by Douglas firs, and sweeping views of the valley. Turning the pictures to the light, I thought I picked out a small stream meandering through a forested glen. The site seemed idyllic.

We flew back to Oregon as soon as Northwest Airlines could get us off the ground. On the plane, I held the photos on my lap. I showed them to the woman sitting next to me; things were looking up. My ex-citement peaked. We unpacked at Steiger Haus in McMinnville, where we were already regulars, as the owners examined the photographs.

"Why can't we see the actual house?" asked Lynn and Doris Steiger. "Where is this place?"

This last question, coming from longtime residents of the small town, unhinged me slightly.

Ron and I shrugged. Near a cherry orchard was all we knew. Somewhere east of town. Somewhere fantastic.

Bewildered, Lynn and Doris shook their heads.

What did they know? Ron and I were champing at the bit to get to this one-of-a-kind place. The property could be snapped up momentarily.

Ginger sped us to the house; the grounds were every bit as inviting as they looked in the pictures. Perfect for garden parties, wine tastings, weddings. The one-story structure was still somewhat difficult to take in, encapsulated in laurel and camellias. I could only imagine the setting at cherry blossom time with petals drifting like pink snow.

As we neared the front door, Ginger sounded the first warning: a wind from the east, a tickle in the throat, a rattle in the refrigerator . . .

"The owners celebrate year-round Christmas," she said. Outside it was early autumn, finches picked at ripe blackberries, and bees hummed in the lavender.

Inside, the smell of bayberry and cinnamon wafted from flickering red candles. Festive swags draped the doorways, and a frenetic train scurried on its tired route through a ceramic Christmas village resting on a blanket of "snow."

I've seen holiday boutiques with fewer ornaments. Beneath the artificial pine boughs, the house's interior—and I'll leave it at this—was not what we'd expected. We dragged back to the car in a wretched state of post-holiday depression. My sneezing turned to wheezing. Ginger suggested that putting new veneers on the kitchen cabinets wouldn't be exorbitantly expensive.

"It's more than the cabinets," I said.

Despite my pessimism, Ginger remained upbeat. "We'll find something," she promised.

"There's no house for us," I sniveled as soon as we returned to the B&B.

"Why don't you buy Steiger Haus?" our hosts asked.

What? Buy Steiger Haus? That would mean the Steigers were moving.

Indeed, they confided they had a dream of building a new inn in eastern Oregon. Now my spirits really plummeted. I'd been counting on Doris and Lynn for long-term friendships.

While I was pulling myself together, Ron nixed the B&B business. For once, I was in full agreement. We still didn't know if we could handle the winery, much less overnight guests.

"Let's just drive by some new construction," Ginger suggested— and we were on the road again.

"Do you like that one?" she asked, pointing toward a new house perched high off the street on a hillside stripped of trees.

"No," I said.

The structure was the color of baloney. Later I discovered the interior (and I mean every room—walls, woodwork, carpet, and ceilings) was done in an even spicier baloney tone.

"No, absolutely not," I repeated.

Within the hour, I surrendered to the lure of sparkling new appliances, sold out to an enormous master bath, and submitted to the convenience of a two-sink kitchen. We bought the baloney house. Ron and Ginger adored the place. Ron maintained that the interior was the color of a low-fat latte, but no one could dispute the exterior. Oscar Mayer.

At least we wouldn't have to move there until spring.

UPSIZING

A festive occasion like buying a new house might call for breaking out a magnum (one and a half liters) of wine. There's cachet in serving a crowd from large format bottles. Magnums are often hand-bottled, and, instead of foiling, the bottle tops are dipped in wax, which can be melted in a tin can on a hotplate. No two handcrafted magnums ever look exactly the same.

A three-liter bottle is called a Jeroboam. If you want a bottle that would hold a full case of wine (imagine pouring from it), or nine liters, look for a Salmanazar.

As Ron puts it, "Split a bottle of wine and you're debonair. Split a Salmanazar and you're dead."

Premium wineries hand sort grapes.

CHAPTER 6

Food Pyramids

OKAY, WHEN WE MOVED to McMinnville we'd have a place to live. Meanwhile, we were still living out of suitcases at the Steigers' B&B. We had to get back to the business of making wine. When I wasn't on the sorting line, I tried to get a handle on food preparation, eventually turning robotic in my chore. Bake and freeze. Bake and freeze: steaks, roasts, chicken, lasagna, spaghetti, sausages, and Tex-Mex casseroles.

Because we never knew precisely when the trucks bearing grapes would show up, Ron and I decided to keep our troops on alert, at the winery. This meant either buying carryout meals or making the food ourselves. After comparing prices and asking around about what other wineries did in this situation, I volunteered to cook. At first I viewed meal preparation, even in the Panther Creek's simple kitchen, as recess from the sorting line.

Little did I know that two meals a day for up to fifteen workers for several weeks could defeat Emeril, Wolfgang Puck, and all the Iron Chefs running a tag team. I felt like the jitterbug chef—dancing from recipe card to cookbook, entrée to dessert. Though I aspired to quality, quantity was my goal. Bake and freeze. Bake and freeze. About a week to ten days into harvest, I folded and resorted to expensive carryout meals. A few of those and I was back to cooking again.

The amount of food that ten to fifteen husky men can put away is staggering. I baked nine pounds of beef brisket one autumn afternoon. The portion proved inadequate for a single meal.

Aha, I thought; I can play this game. The following day I roasted three turkeys. The turkeys had actually been thawing for the better part of a week in the refrigerator. (Anticipation is part of the jitterbug chef's job description.) Unfortunately, I hadn't counted on the fact that vast quantities of frozen meat create a refrigerator tundra, making defrosting next to impossible. My lettuce froze; my milk iced over; and my birds were still stiffs, despite several cool baths, when I loaded them into the oven.

I began with two turkeys at three hundred fifty degrees. Many hours later, the little rascals browned up and cooked through. After carving turkeys one and two and returning them to the tundra, I slipped number three in the oven. Later that afternoon, I ran to the grocery store to stock up on ever more provisions. While I waited at the deli counter, another shopper came up behind me. McMinnville is made up of a wide range of individuals—including a small but thriving artistic community. The "artiste" behind me at the deli counter tapped her foot until she caught the eye of a clerk.

"I'm going to have some of that turkey. It smells delicious," she said.

"We don't have turkey," announced the clerk. "Vegetarian lasagna, meat loaf, or fried chicken. That's it."

Less cordial now, the customer impatiently shoved her bracelet up her arm and readjusted her paisley shawl. Coiffed and manicured, she looked as if she'd darted into the grocery store on her way home from a soiree. The woman snorted her displeasure at the day's deli selections.

"I can smell the turkey," she insisted.

As subtly as I could, I sniffed the arm of my sweatshirt.

It was then that I realized the exhaust from my oven had permeated my clothes and hung like a cloud in my hair. Embarrassed, the jitterbug chef grabbed her cheese and ran.

Fortunately, the turkey lasted several days at the winery—or until we ran afoul of fowl, if you know what I mean. Bake and freeze.

Given a choice, the men eat from the pinnacle of the food pyramid. They fancy dishes like brisket, basically rich meats and gravies. When I pointed out this serious breach of nutritional dictum, Ben, a part-timer with an appetite for barbecued pork and meat loaf crisscrossed with pepper bacon, cracked us up by saying he considered the lower levels of the pyramid to be nothing more than condiments. I've learned that serving "condiments," like arugula salads and broccoli, is just a waste of good greens. I don't especially love marathon cooking, but my coworkers are so complimentary that food preparation is worth the effort.

Sometimes volunteers who yearn for the crush experience or others who want to learn more about winemaking show up unexpectedly—at least, unexpectedly to me—during harvest. In most cases volunteers make life easier for those who have been working around the clock. If a volunteer is sorting on the line, obviously, the only courteous thing to do is feed him or her with the rest of the crew.

Ron met me at the winery door late one afternoon.

"How many tenderloins did you buy for dinner?" he asked. I was weighted down with grocery store bags, which he took from my arms.

"Six," I said as we headed toward the kitchen. "I'm going to grill them."

"Can we get more?" Ron asked. I began counting workers on my fingers.

"There are some volunteers staying for dinner," he continued. Ron pointed toward the back room. I recognized one of the guys as a well-known Portland chef. He was young, but already creating a stir in Portland culinary circles.

"He's eating here?" I asked, trying to calm myself, thinking Zen-like thoughts: streams flowing, leaves fluttering, clouds floating. Back to reality, I quickly reviewed the menu in my mind: pork tenderloin, French bread, and roasted vegetables. The food was straightforward, but this was to be my first attempt at *grilled* tenderloins. I was comfortable with the gas Weber we used at home, but a vintage charcoal grill was all that existed at the winery. Its air vents were grease-locked in open positions. I cringed at the thought of cooking for the chef and his friend. Maybe we could still order carryout. I suggested saving the meat for the next night.

"He's looking forward to pork tenderloin," Ron said. The chef caught my eye and waved from the back room. I waved back, trying to look confident. His restaurant featured the best Northwest seasonal cuisine: truffles, wild mushrooms, smoked sturgeon, that sort of thing.

"Okay," I said. "I just hope you didn't say anything that would heighten his expectations."

"Only that it's good," Ron admitted.

Slightly peeved at that endorsement, I gathered my ingredients. At least I'd purchased the vegetables at the farmer's market: regular carrots and some that were a new exotic yellow, parsnips, fennel, and red potatoes.

That evening, as I could have predicted, the fire in the grill refused to settle down. Every time I cracked open the lid the coals flared like an eruption on the sun—although dusk had evolved into a starless, moonless night and my grilling zone was pitch black. The grill, hot as a meteorite entering our atmosphere, couldn't be budged to a more convenient work area.

Finally, fearing the coals would burn themselves out before the flames died down, I teetered out of the kitchen balancing (now) eight pork tenderloins and rolled them on to the rack. At first they sizzled, then they sparked, and then they stuck. Flames of fire rose from the grill, causing a vague murmur from the sorting line. I jumped back to avoid self-incineration.

The chef wandered over. The hair on my right arm felt singed.

"This meat's going to ignite before it cooks through," I said, rubbing my arm. The pork was on the grill, but I was in the pressure cooker.

"Nah," he said. "It's seared perfectly. Just push the tenderloins toward the outside of the fire."

"Oh," I said, brightening. Perhaps dinner could be salvaged after all.

The chef drifted back to his place on the line. Diving into the smoke, I realigned the tenderloins, which had miraculously unstuck themselves from the rack. Then I rushed to the kitchen to check on the vegetables.

Minutes later, I was grilling again. The chef wandered back. "If I had a flashlight," I said, "I'd know when they were done."

He poked at the meat with his finger. His face glowed like a moon above the fire.

"Five minutes," he said, sensing the cooking temperature of the pork by feel. I sprinkled salt and pepper, then spread a secret ingredient—okay, apricot jelly—over the roasts. Five minutes later I lay eight sizzling pork tenderloins on the table.

I'm not one to brag about my cooking, but this near catastrophe emerged as one of my all-time best meals. Everyone except the chef had seconds; I couldn't help but notice that he took thirds. For once the guys devoured the roasted vegetables, going so far as to rave about their freshness.

"It must be those yellow carrots from the farmer's market," I said. I tried to catch our chef-volunteer's eye to relay my thanks, but he was distracted, asking if anybody was going to eat that last slice of pork.

Just then we heard a clatter from the back and a heavyset truck driver in slid-down jeans and a shrunken T-shirt wandered toward the table.

"You guys order a stainless fermenting tank from California?" he asked.

Yes, we did. Yes, we did. Yes, we did. The lost was found and life was good again.

We eat—sometimes we linger at the table, other times we gulp our dinners—and then we crush. The grapes dictate our eating, sleeping, and work. Fruit rules.

2,300 gallon tanks with refrigeration capabilities are used to ferment red wine.

 CHAPTER 7

Fear and Fermentation

RON AND I SHUFFLED from our car toward the Union Block Coffee Shop in downtown McMinnville with the effects of too many predawn bedtimes showing in our middle-aged bodies. I recited a silent mantra in my brain. "Single latte, double latte, triple latte, now."

On the weary scale, everyone at the winery now ranked somewhere between run-down and whipped. As harvest passed, fleeting aches and pains materialized, then evaporated—only to bring on new afflictions. That day my back had a crick from standing on the sorting line and my eyeballs ached from fatigue. Outside of gardening, physical labor had never been my forte. Dale, our veteran of many harvests, revealed he'd prepared for the rigors of the conveyor belt at the gym.

Hard to believe, but I looked worse than I felt—as if I'd landed on painful Planet Purple. I'd Cloroxed my hands, but the grapes continued to arrive at the winery, and once again I was gloved in the color of fresh bruises. Noting the detrimental impact on my fingernails, I'd decided to wait until I was certain crush was over before attempting a second bleach manicure. I recalled the days back in Iowa when I'd occasionally indulged in beauty shop manicures. I drew a self-indulgent breath at the thought of someone massaging lotion into my lavender cuticles.

We'd lost track of the exact date, but a glance at the calendar on my checkbook cover revealed we were already halfway through October. Night temperatures were crawling toward the freeze mark, but days were still dry and sunny—ideal harvest conditions. Fermentation was at hand and pressing would follow: before wine can be barreled, seeds, skins, and pulp must be pressed off.

Union Block Coffee Shop is located halfway between Steiger Haus and Panther Creek. Ron and I picked up our shuffle and trotted around the corner toward our destination. The smell of roasted beans usually greeted us at the door, but that Sunday morning another aroma streamed through the air near the coffee shop. We stopped short.

"What's that?" I whispered, knowing, but afraid of the answer. A yeast-y, ferment-y, and very familiar scent clobbered our nostrils.

Fear darkened Ron's eyes. Without another word, we turned and ran back to the car. More than fifty tons of grapes were "cooking" in our tanks. The byproducts of fermentation are a dynamic duo, heat and carbon dioxide. Ron was thinking leak: I was thinking explosion.

We spun around corners at high speed and revved the engine on the straightaways past the jail, over the railroad tracks, and on to the front of the winery. Our car scraped the curb and jolted to a stop.

Both of us had envisioned the worst, but wine was not spewing from under the front door. The sidewalk looked dry. A peek inside revealed everything in order. Apparently all the wineries in McMinnville were simultaneously experiencing fermentation, which resulted in some very potent aromas wafting through town.

Weak with exhaustion and caffeine deprivation, we laughed out loud at our jitters. Every time Ron touched me, I laughed harder. We collapsed on the sidewalk, resting our backs on the winery doors until we could collect ourselves.

That episode probably made us less wary, even a little cocky. I won't say we hadn't been warned. In a winery, heat and carbon dioxide can work for you—or against you.

The dreaded overflow actually happened a few days later. Our stainless steel tanks hold approximately 2,300 gallons. Unlike a common coffeemaker, the tanks aren't marked with a red warning line indicating when to stop filling. Liquid and solid matter are put directly into the tanks after the grapes are crushed. The intensity (in this case, I'm referring to the speed of the fermentation) and the amount of seeds, skin, and pulp in the juice that will become wine determines the space required in the tank. Fermentation is the process of changing sugar to alcohol and—as I just mentioned—the byproducts of fermentation are carbon dioxide and heat. During fermentation, carbon dioxide causes movement in the juice, sort of like the fizz in a Coke, and the solids (or cap) get pushed to the top of the tank.

In our overflow situation, the cap looked like a coarse, purple souffle swelling ominously above the top of one of our large tanks. We watched the monstrosity grow, inch by inch. If only it had been a scene from *I Love Lucy* instead of real life.

Not once, but two days in a row, the cap rose and collapsed down the outside of the tank. Unfortunately, a tank that holds 2,300 gallons is more difficult to clean than a coffeemaker. Oozy muck clung on the refrigeration blanket, covered the ladder, enveloped the thermometer, slimed the door, and fused on the valves; then the overflow seeped into purple puddles on the floor.

We couldn't just hose all those expensive skins and seeds down the drain. The disgorged solids were still necessary for the color and flavor they impart to the wine. The guys not only cleaned up the mess and re-covered what they could of the solids, but they also racked (moved) some of the wine from the overflow tank into a clean tank. Then they had to figure a logical ratio of cap to liquid and add an appropriate amount of the salvaged seeds and skins to the wine in the new tank. Here's my second axiom of the universe: Sticky situations like this only occur when people are already frazzled.

Someone has said that ninety percent of winemaking is cleanup. All the equipment, the walls, the crush pad, the drains, and the tarmac out behind the winery must be hosed down at the very minimum before we finish for the night. The washing (no soap), scrubbing, sweeping, and squeegeeing take at least an hour, sometimes nearly two. If a single load of grapes is crushed in the early afternoon and a second load doesn't arrive until evening, we clean everything in between. If we were to wait until the skins, grapes, and juice that are smashed on the floor, stuck in the conveyor, or smattered on the side of the destemmer were dry, cleanup would have to be done with chisels.

The final act every night involves hosing one another down. Each of us wears waterproof bib-overalls and rubber boots. That first year we tried to remember to pull off our boots whenever we left the crush room. The ban on boots through the winery supposedly eliminated sticky paths, specifically between the work area and the kitchen and/or the bathroom. Naturally, the restriction proved impossible; juice and grape skins couldn't be prevented from seeping throughout the entire building. We forgot, emergencies happened, phones rang; friends, volunteers, truck drivers, the mailman, vineyard owners, and customers trudged through the crush room and into the winery. Eventually the whole place had to be hosed down and scrubbed up anyway.

The winery looks and smells fresh late at night when the walls stream with clean water, the drains are freed of skins and stems, and the machines sparkle. With the physical labor behind us, I actually enjoy driving toward a soft bed at two or three in the morning. The night air, still salty from the Pacific Ocean just thirty-five miles away, and the abrupt silence revive me. McMinnville looks unfamiliar in lanky shadows thrown by trees and grain elevators. Streetlights and ginkgo leaves flutter yellow. City streets are quiet; even Highway 99 is deserted. At least, mostly deserted.

After the bars close, only wildlife roams the streets. Once in the wee hours, I slammed on my brakes for a rat the size of a Chihuahua darting through the glare of my headlights. I rubbed my eyes and watched as the beast—I'm terrified of rats—leapt up over the curb, sprinted across the sidewalk, and crashed headlong into the brick building on the far side of Fourth Street. The sight was so grotesque, I pulled over and waited to see if the rodent would recover. He was still out cold on the sidewalk when I finally drove away. The next day my first words to the guys were a warning about closing the doors as soon as we finished. We're not interested in four-footed visitors.

Sleep comes easily during harvest. I have a recurring dream of grapes passing rhythmically on a conveyor. Ron, on the other hand, uses the hours for worry. He worries about the price of the grapes, the quality of the grapes, winemaking techniques, marketing issues, and safety. Actually, we both worry about safety.

Though there's adequate space in a third-floor loft, no one ever sleeps at the winery because of the risk of asphyxiation. The carbon dioxide emitted during fermentation can displace the oxygen in the air and enter the human lung so insidiously that workers have suffocated in wineries. Crush can be lethal. At Panther Creek, timed fans suck out the carbon dioxide before workers arrive in the morning.

I climbed the stairs to the second-floor offices at the winery one morning after surviving a drilling in the dentist's chair. (The good news was I'd found a dentist in McMinnville. The bad news was he concurred with my Des Moines dentist about my needing three crowns.) Though it was still early, Ron was already at work, and I began rifling through a stack of *Wine Spectator*'s on his desk.

Suddenly my head felt v-e-r-y heavy. Had the *Spectator* given that Cabernet an 83 or an 88? My eyes wouldn't focus.

"I didn't feel dizzy at the dentist's, but I do now," I told Ron in puffs.

He pushed away from his desk and dragged me down the stairs and outside.

"I'm feeling woozy too," he admitted. Carbon dioxide is lethal and sneaky. We opened both the garage doors at the back of the building and the door in front. By the time Michael and Jack arrived, the gas had dissipated and Ron and I were back to normal. That was a close call we hoped not to repeat.

During fermentation the cap that carbon dioxide pushes to the top of the wine must be punched back into the liquid at least once a day. Contact with the grape skins and pulp improves the color and the flavor of the finished product. This job requires strength, balance, dexterity, and acumen. Consequently, I've never been asked to punch down. Sometimes the cap is so thick a person can stand on it, even jump on it.

At the moment the cap is broken, carbon dioxide rushes out of the fermenting wine. The unwary worker struggling with the cap could collapse and fall onto the cement floor ten feet below or, more deadly, into the tank of wine where drowning is a real possibility. If a person passes out into a 2,300-gallon tank filled with approximately eight feet of warm, fermenting wine, he or she will quickly drown.

Unfortunately, most cellar workers I've known resist oxygen tanks because of the extra weight and the fact they dislike the inconvenience of being tethered to a harness, though Ron and I recommend it. Only wineries using completely mechanized punching-down devices that run on tracks above the tanks are free of this danger.

Wine, however, is a living, changing organism, and rough treatment ruins it. Unfortunately, fragile Pinot Noirs usually can't stand up to mechanical punching down. For all these reasons, we've initiated a policy of using spotters to keep an eye on cellar workers while they're working in that dangerous zone at the top of the wine tanks.

Although I've never punched down, I have served as spotter, a job similar to lifeguarding at a swimming pool. Many lunch discussions center around the scenario of how a spotter should react if a person faints into the tank. The only solid decision we've made is *not* to open the porthole-sized door on the front of the tanks. (The cellar workers use this opening for cleaning when the tank is empty.) According to current thinking, the victim would be sucked deeper into the wine if the door is opened.

Even after all our conversations, my reaction was terror when a cellar worker slipped into the drink on my watch. It was James, a part-timer from a culinary school who had appeared on our doorstep wanting to learn the ins and outs of winemaking.

I'd been absorbed in my own thoughts, never dreaming the worst. I saw him go straight down and then slip beneath the lip of the tank. Seconds passed; my throat and legs felt paralyzed. When I could move, I ran to the tank, knowing it brimmed with Pinot Noir. Screaming for the other guys, I had just started toward the ladder when James's head appeared over the top.

"I slipped," he said, disgusted with himself. James didn't faint—but technically, medically, I didn't care *why* he fell in.

"Get out fast," I ordered, not because he was contaminating the wine (highly alcoholic), but because our friend was still in danger of carbon dioxide suffocation.

James groaned as he wrenched himself out of the liquid and climbed down from the tank. Purple from head to toe, he had grape skins dangling from every protuberance. He was so furious at himself that when he touched terra firma, he shook like a dog, flinging skins high and low. I could only stare. He walked directly out of the winery, into the street, and toward—I presume—a shower. Somewhere. I just stood near the tank with my mouth still hanging open and my heart whacking in my chest. James appeared again later that day, scrubbed and clean, and in a much improved state of mind. No one mentioned "the incident." We were just thankful he lived *not* to tell about it.

Wine Notes:

HARVEST HITCHHIKERS, WILD YEASTS

Wine in the tanks undergoes fermentation because of yeasts. Yeasts are the organisms that turn sugar to alcohol. Appropriate yeasts accentuate qualities of a particular wine; they also strongly influence the speed, intensity, and quality of fermentation.

Native yeasts hitch a ride into the winery on the grapes that come in from established vineyards. Then these "wild things" hang around in the winery, vintage after vintage. I don't know if they're lying on the brick wall, embedded in the barrels, or swinging off the ceiling—but they're around. This is also true in bakeries, and it's one reason that wineries and bakeries create products with distinctive flavor profiles.

Many first-rate wineries let nature, in the form of native yeasts, take its course. We, however, believe in minimal intervention, because when things get "too wild," we get nervous. We intervene by adding purchased, or proprietary, yeasts. The proprietary yeasts take over the fermentation, yet allow native strains to put their mark on the wine. Ideally, we choose yeasts that complement a vineyard's characteristics. In other words, we look for yeasts that accentuate the strengths of the grapes and minimize, or shore up, their weaknesses. Some yeasts enhance aromatics, some build texture, and so on.

Once fermentation begins, we add a yeast-nutrient mixture that keeps the yeasts healthy while they do their work. If you fail to add nutrients, yeasts can produce compounds that create off-aromas in the wine.

If this sounds precise, it's not. Wild or native yeasts and cross inoculation multiply the variables dizzyingly.

I learned that even similar-sized tanks of wine ferment at different speeds. When carbon dioxide no longer supports the cap and the seeds and skins drift to the bottom of the tank, fermentation is complete. Some tanks still need to be punched down while others have completed that step and are ready for pressing.

Weeks before when Dale had first explained the process of turning grapes to wine, I never imagined pressing would turn into the most physically grueling part of crush. That first crush, every gallon of new wine had to be tediously pumped into one of two antique-looking basket presses that separate the skins, pulp, and seeds from the wine.

Each wine press was the size of a wine barrel (a barrel contains approximately twenty-four cases of wine); each contained a flexible rubber bladder that expanded to push the wine and solids against the side of the basket. A few gallons were pumped into the press; the cellar workers would slowly expand the bladder against the sides of the basket so the wine trickled away from the solids; and then Mark tasted what ran out. The winemaker has to determine when to stop pressing. Pressing the solids too dry makes the finished wine extremely tannic. Strong tannins leave a taster's mouth with that uncomfortable puckery feeling. By the way, if a winemaker swallowed the wine he tastes during these pressings, he or she would be in terrible shape by the end of harvest. Most wineries, ours included, have grates in the floor that are used for spitting.

The guys repeated the process again and again until most of the wine was pressed. After pressing, the solids (pomace) remained inside the basket; the wine that trickled out the bottom of the basket was captured in a metal tray. Then the wine was gently pumped (racked) into a clean tank.

The bricks of pomace from every pressing had to be broken up by hand and carried away by the armload. I wondered if the pressing would be completed before the next vintage began.

Thousands of gallons of wine were pushed through those small presses. The young Pinot Noir ran thick and red as blood. Mark tasted—and spit—after every pressing, ascertaining that the pressure in the baskets wasn't creating too tannic a product. You can read about balancing tannins in manuals or learn about it in seminars, but only experience teaches a winemaker this skill. Tannins are the chemicals that allow wine to age well—but young, strong tannins can also create an uncomfortable dry feeling on the palate. Tannins either enhance the wine or dominate it.

Wine Notes:

LET'S TALK TANNINS

❧

Beginning tasters can be put off by the dry, puckery sensation of tannins on their palates. At worst, tannins make your mouth feel chalky or dusty. Yet experienced tasters know balanced tannins portend a good, or possibly a great, wine. Some terroirs (conditions in the vineyard) produce more tannic wines than others.

A red wine with few tannins is called soft; fruitiness predominates in these wines. Sometimes they're made this way to be drunk without benefit of bottle aging. Do you know the joke about how Americans age wine? They buy a bottle on Wednesday and wait all the way to Saturday to serve it.

The guys in our winery call soft wines "slutty" because their fruitiness makes the wines easy, seductive, and often best-sellers when they're young. Unfortunately, these wines don't age particularly well or become particularly interesting because they have so little going on structurally. Just like their human counterpoints, wines need a backbone. Something to support that fruit.

Tannins are a vital element of fine red wines. Combined with acid and fruitiness, tannins add balance. The best wines, ones that age in the barrel and continue to improve in the bottle, offer a complex array of pleasant flavors and aromas. Without tannins, complexity becomes nonexistent. Winemakers and folks who buy Pinot Noir futures at barrel tastings judge aging potential in part by the wine's tannins.

Tannins get into the wine when the juice or wine comes in contact with stems, skins, and seeds. White wines, which are made without grape-skin contact, offer few tannins. (White-wine grapes are crushed, pressed, and fermented; red-wine grapes are crushed, fermented, and then pressed.)

When the solid materials soak (macerate) in the juice or wine, the wine gains tannins. And, when the pulp is pressed away from the wine, it receives another good shot of tannins. A young wine with extremely strong tannins may take longer to come around—or reach its peak balance.

During sorting, fermentation, and even pressing, visitors roamed in and out of the winery. Although we didn't have a tasting room, Ron was eager to attract outsiders, thinking they would create excitement about our product. I supposed he was right.

Because wine hadn't been my passion back in Des Moines, or even a passing interest, I have to say it surprised me to think that people would want to visit the cellar. I would have understood if Panther Creek had a tasting room, but we didn't. These people were interested in watching us process the grapes.

During all the years of our marriage, I'd only visited Ron in his law offices on occasions such as the signing of our wills. Much as he welcomed me and encouraged my visits, I always felt like an interloper in his work lair. Somewhere along the line I'd gotten the idea that it wasn't a good thing to turn up at factories, warehouses, labs, and offices unless you were there on business. Initially I didn't see why visitors, who seemed friendly and thoughtful, kept appearing at our winery door. They could, after all, buy our wine at numerous shops. I liked Coach purses, but I'd never thought of traveling to the factory to see how the leather was stitched together.

After a lot of thought I did recall a visit to a perfume factory where the girls and I had dragged Ron near the town of Grasse, France. High in the cliffs above the Mediterranean, the factory stood in a manicured field striped with lavender plants. A factory representative gave us the modified tour, which meant we didn't see any of the crew using the machinery. Our guide told us how their workers could take a ton of lavender and turn it into a dram (not exact measurements) of the finest perfume. The girls and I raised our eyebrows in amazement. I'd really hoped to meet the nose—the person with unusually heightened olfactory capabilities whose purpose it is to develop, sniffing out and blending, new fragrances. Later it dawned on me that the nose of the perfume factory, with his sensational schnoz, was the winemaker's counterpart. The winemaker depends primarily on his or her palate, though the sense of smell is also vital, especially when it comes to di-agnosing problem wines.

In thinking back, I decided how much more interesting the per-fume factory would have been if we'd seen the workers crushing the lavender. I wished the nose had been sniffing around. The French per-fume factory helped me figure out what visitors enjoy at the winery. In truth, however, the visitors to both places seek that which can't be seen: the magic of turning the mundane into the magnificent.

A high school algebra teacher—a sturdy string bean in a striped shirtwaist who was also bunking at Steiger's B&B—asked one morning over a bowl of Doris's homemade granola if I gave winery tours.

"A tour?" I repeated. "For you, sure."

Even as I greeted her at Panther Creek a few hours later, the schoolteacher began asking awkward questions. Stressed, my brain immediately erased everything Dale had taught me.

Looking back, the algebra teacher sounded something like this: "If a five-ton truck fully loaded with grapes started out from Freedom Hill Vineyard and a two-ton truck started from Shea Vineyard thirty miles apart at the exactly same time, and if each traveled at exactly the same speed, would the drivers recognize each other when they got to the winery?" My God, I never thought about it.

She pointed to a chain hanging from the ceiling. "And what's that for?"

"Pressing," I ventured.

"How's it work?"

I didn't know. "Oh, yes, I think they hang the lid of the barrel press on the chain while they clean the skins and seeds from the barrel. Yes, that's it." Or was it? I couldn't remember. In fact, I'd never noticed the chain until she pointed it out. I'd watched Ron give tours. No one asked *him* crazy questions.

Fortunately, a painter was working on a ladder high above the crush room. Noting my discomfort, the painter began miming the answers to the schoolteacher's questions.

"I've always wondered," she asked, "is it possible to make white wine from red grapes?"

I glanced upward. The painter gave a quick nod.

"Yes," I said. "You can, but it's complicated." Then I hustled into subjects I understood. I found that if I spoke at full tilt, she didn't have time to throw out random queries.

When I'd completed my tour and escorted the teacher to the door, she said, "I hope you appreciate what you've got here."

I think she meant the winery, but at that moment I was appreciating the guy on the ladder.

The most ominous question came from my own father a short time later. My sister brought him to McMinnville for a visit, so, of course, I hauled them both over to Panther Creek as soon as they stepped into town. Beth had the normal inquiries: "Why do you sort the grapes? How long do you keep the wine in barrels?"

Dad was waiting for his moment. "At what point do you wash the grapes?" he asked.

Because I knew he wasn't going to like the answer, I ignored the interruption and tried to move my explanation to the area of grape sorting.

"We take out mold, leaves, and any grapes that might not be ripe," I said, pointing toward the ultra-clean conveyor belt.

"But when do you wash the grapes?" he repeated a second, then a third time. I could tell by Beth's grimace that she, too, sensed I was try-ing to change the subject.

"We don't," I admitted at last.

"You don't wash the grapes?" His mouth dropped open in disbelief.

"No."

"Never?"

"No."

He shook his head.

I thought back to a junior high social studies project about Hawaii. There are ten steps to refining sugar. Do you know what the first one is? Washing the canes, of course. I stammered around until I remem-bered something important Dale had told me about winemaking.

"If the grapes get soaked, we'll end up with watery wine," I said. Dale had actually been referring to rain-wet fruit, but the fact seemed to fit.

I could tell by my dad's crossed arms that he wasn't buying it. Everyone washes fruit before eating it.

At last my brain focused; I found my edge. "We're making alcohol here. Alcohol kills germs. You don't *have* to wash the grapes." I watched my dad's face relax. He'd actually bought my explanation. My own shoulders slumped in relief.

Suddenly he blurted, "So what's the purpose of this chain?" Of all the equipment and processes used in winemaking, that dangling chain used to hang the press lids held the most mystique for our visitors. At least on my tours.

Close-up of pinot noir. Pickers remove leaves and other debris before the grapes get to the winery.

 CHAPTER 8

Social Insecurity

I F I SOUND AS IF that first harvest was all work—sorting grapes, feeding the crew, and giving tours—that would be untrue. We'd begun to have a little social life in wine country. Early on, however, I'd worried if we'd ever fit in.

To add to my apprehension, I watched a show on cable about a French couple who had purchased a winery in, I believe, Bordeaux. This program, which was probably a yawn for most of the world's population, mesmerized me. The new couple was required—*mais oui*, this was Bordeaux—to host the neighboring vintners at a bash rivaling America's annual New Year's Eve celebration in Times Square. The skittish hostess spent months interviewing top-drawer caterers, florists, and musicians. After much hand-wringing she decided on a large tent with a dance floor on the grounds of their *beau château*. The antiquity, the countryside, the vines: what a backdrop! Except that on the day of the party, with hundreds of guests treading up the cobblestone drive, the heavens opened and poured buckets. The hostess stood near a tent stay and tried to collect herself as her drippy guests decided they were too chilled to hang around for dinner. My God, I thought, don't leave now, she's arranged for sauteed sweetbreads, goose pâté, blood pudding, or some other darn thing. The new couple had coughed up a million dollars for the event, not to mention what they'd laid out on the vineyards and winery. I felt like writing the poor woman a condolence note.

The reporter didn't conclude with anything to the effect, "Despite nature's caprice, these vintners eventually fit in with their neighbors." No, the viewer was left with the conclusion that this initial bad impression, a form of cursed karma, had shattered these investors' chances of ever finding any success in the Bordeaux business. *Quelle misère!*

While the Oregon wine social scene couldn't be further from what I'd seen on television, that first year Panther Creek received a devastating blow with the potential for such tremendous negative ramifications that I questioned the status of our karma in the universe—at least, in the universe of fine wine.

Enthusiastic about putting his best foot forward in the Pinot Noir community, Ron had entered one of our wines in a lavish annual festival held on the Linfield College campus in McMinnville. Gourmands and wine lovers from all over the world converge annually for a weekend of fabulous Pinot Noir, fine food prepared by esteemed chefs, and the opportunity to hobnob with vintners from as far away as Burgundy, Chile, and even Tasmania. Because we were one of a handful of hometown wineries, Ron was eager to participate in an event that garners positive publicity. (The festival was often featured in front-page articles in publications as far-reaching as *USA Today*.)

Space limitations allowed only six hundred, lottery-winning guests who forked out about $600 each to participate. Wineries wishing to pour their wine at the event were required to submit a sample to be subjected to a blind, critical tasting. Ron, certain he had a winner and hoping to represent Panther Creek at the event, had offered up our Pinot Noir on the appointed day. The wine was characteristic of a notable vintage and typical of what we now recognize as Shea Vineyard fruit: a bright-tasting young wine, brimming with red berry flavors that would be made even more interesting with cellaring.

Weeks later, Ron was shattered to learn Panther Creek's Shea Vineyard Pinot Noir had been rejected by the festival panel. When he came into the kitchen that night, I could tell by the set of my husband's jaw that something devastating had happened. Something he really didn't even want to discuss, especially with me. At last I wrenched the story of the rejection from him: Ron said that even though some of the blind tasters were new friends and regretted the outcome, they were sticking by their palates. Panther Creek would not be participating in the festival unless Ron and I were prepared to spend $600 each; enter and win lottery tickets; and come as guests, not as vintners. More than the words, I heard the defeat in Ron's voice.

I didn't say so then, but this cinched it: I was terrified we'd made a mistake in buying the winery. Perhaps winemaking was a skill, if not an art, we'd never master. Perhaps we'd lose our investment, which was also our retirement fund. The rejection stung and the fear festered.

It wasn't long, however, until I discovered that our fellow vintners were nothing like their French-televised counterparts; our new colleagues were going out of their way to be congenial. Even while we were still commuting between Iowa and Oregon, Ron and I were invited to a dinner party arranged by Mark, Panther Creek's winemaker, and his wife.

Because we were living out of a suitcase, I'd packed just one dressy outfit for the trip, anticipating the vast majority of my time would be spent in jeans doing winery work. So, when Mark said he wanted us to meet his wine friends, I re-Cloroxed my hands and felt fortunate to happen on the dress in my suitcase. The date was late October and the long-sleeved outfit was constructed of some sort of unfortunate thermal fabric. I hadn't realized when I packed back home that summer temperatures can molder in the Willamette Valley all fall.

It didn't help that Ron and I had been in a vineyard earlier that afternoon, and because we were already halfway to Salem where the party was to be held, I was forced to change into my off-white outfit—which was ideal for attracting permanent stains—in a park restroom. (Try twisting into nylons without touching a toe on the slimy floor or a finger on the grimy wall.) Although the restroom could have doubled as a convection oven, I had at least remembered everything—from hairbrush to shoes—needed for a head-to-toe transformation.

Mark grilled salmon that evening. I recall heaping potluck platters of tomatoes, mozzarella, and basil, accompanied by baguettes, potato salad, cheesecake, and several dozen bottles of open Pinot Noir lined up in the center of the Vlossaks' expanded trestle dining table. I also remember the intensity of the heat and feeling slightly giddy. By the way people were chattering, I sensed they'd been friends, as well as colleagues, for decades.

As we sat down to dinner, sweat trickled down my forehead, broke out on my back, and ran rivulets down my legs. Adding to the burden of trying to appear gracious, witty, smart, and attractive was my thermal, waffle-weave dress. I felt as parboiled as the potatoes. A lone fan cooled guests at the far end of the table. Noticing my distress, our hostess casually repositioned the fan so it blew squarely between my shoulder blades. My hair ruffed but the sensation was so pleasant I closed my eyes and thanked the saint of collected composure. Between the antihistamines and the heat, I had been passing on the wine. Then it dawned on me that I was dining with the producers of the bottles on the table. They were scrutinizing me.

One of my dinner partners, Dan Dusschee, owner of Freedom Hill Vineyards, looked concerned. "Do you like Pinot Noir?" he whispered.

"Oh, yes," I said, and by then I'd tasted enough to know I really did. "It's just that I'm so warm." I sipped a little and began to feel . . . no ill effects. I wondered which individuals had produced which wines. The fan droned, sunlight slipped to shade, and the wine began to have a desirable effect. So I sipped a little more . . . and began to have some fun. My head cleared, my eyes stopped itching. Believe it or not, I chilled.

After we knew each other better, one of the other vintners told me they had eagerly accepted the invitation to that dinner party because they were very interested in us. For years the Oregon wine community consisted of a stable group of producers, and then suddenly a new wave of faces from all over the world had begun appearing in Willamette Valley vineyards. The established vintners wondered what personalities they would be encountering.

"It was as if a person picked up our deck of cards," one of the vintners explained later, "and threw them up in the air. We didn't know how they'd land." Looking back, I find it peculiar to think the others were anxious too.

Soon after that dinner, we were invited to a get-together given by Panther Creek's founder and previous owner Ken Wright and his wife Karen. I'd heard invitations to their parties were a prized commodity, so we felt flattered to be included. Enticing aromas of everything from steaks to Pinot-spiked sausages hovered in the still air when we arrived at the Wrights' country home. Cars were parked double the length of a football field up and down the lane. Long tables sat outside on the patio; and as at the Vlossaks', they all but sagged with extravagant potluck dishes and dozens of open bottles of Willamette Valley wines. My thermal dress, though frumpy, proved ideal for that evening's more seasonal outdoor temperatures. The excitement heated up after dinner, when Karen and Ken pumped up the rock and roll for dancing. Sparks from the grill snapped and flew skyward like a miniature burst of fireworks. The music throbbed. Among the guests, I recognized some people we'd already met in McMinnville—like Dale and his woman friend. I met the cousin of a Des Moines acquaintance and had to smile at the similarity of their mannerisms.

Next thing I knew, a couple of grape growers jumped on one of the tables and started to swing. Her shoes pounded out the beat and his heels ground into the tabletop. Partygoers grabbed for their glasses, leaving only the dancers and the flatware to jump in rhythm. Wow, I thought. They didn't dance like *that* in Iowa. And from what I'd seen on television, I guessed they didn't boogie in Bordeaux either.

Barrel heads offer a code to guide the winemaker.

CHAPTER 9

Barreling Along

THAT FIRST FALL Ron decided we should taste the previous years' wines. We were making new wine while the preceding vintage, which we'd purchased from Ken Wright, was still aging in barrel. The prospect of tasting was exciting because we didn't know precisely what each barrel had in store for us, or how the wine we'd purchased was progressing. In a corner here or there we discovered a few mystery barrels, though we were certain some held topping wine.

Topping wine is used to replace the wine that evaporates through the cracks between the barrels' wooden staves. Barrels should be completely full, to limit the wine's contact with oxygen that causes quick aging and spoilage. Yet even with great planning, no vintner could exactly fill all the barrels with wine; harvest always ends with a few partial barrels of leftover wine. These leftover portions of wine are also barreled and then gassed with a nonreactive (inert) gas to prevent their coming in contact with oxygen. Then, as evaporation causes the levels to drop in the full barrels, the winemaker refills them with the wine from the partial (topping) barrels. Not enough wine is transferred from one barrel to another to influence the flavor profile of the finished product, though sanitation is critical.

In an upright position, the barrels stand about waist high. I can't put my arms completely around a barrel (no human could), and I'm not strong enough to roll one without disastrous consequences (although most men could). By disastrous consequences I mean that I might be able to get a barrel moving—but I'd never be able to stop it. The barrels are created by coopers who piece together staves (long, thin pieces of wood) that are held in place with metal belts. The staves, which bulge to make the middle of the barrel fatter than its ends, fit together exactly without glue, nails, or screws. The ends (heads) of the barrels are about the size and shape of manhole covers. The stopper that fits in the hole on the barrel's side is called a bung.

Evaporated wine is romantically referred to as the *angels' share*, a term that harkens back to monastic wineries. The association between monks and vintners dates at least back to the Middle Ages when monks exacted "tithes" from parishioners in the form of property, including vineyards.

In the winery the French oak barrels we purchased were stacked on each other in long rows along the inside walls. The setup was precarious; the slightest earthquake tremor could have sent them careening. Even the vibrations from passing trains made me jittery, so Ron immediately ordered the most "earthquake-tolerant" racks he could locate.

The question remains: In the event of a significant earthquake, would the barrel racks stand as the 1923 brick building collapsed around them? I'd come to grips with Iowa tornadoes, but earthquakes? Any Iowan can tell you that in addition to red blotches on television's Doppler radar, a yellow-green sky and an eerie stillness bode twisters on the horizon. I asked a native Oregonian if a person could predict an earthquake.

"Sure thing," he said. "When all your dogs and cats want to go outside and the cows and horses want to come in." Ron and I had one cat, Chester, who lived to slip outside. He'd be a useless indicator.

Back among the barrel racks, I picked up a glass with Mark, Michael, and Ron. Mark dipped into the barrels with a tool that looks like a bent turkey baster, called a wine thief, and dribbled wine into our glasses. I tasted, sniffed, swirled, and held my own for the first five barrels. We were thrilled at the wine we'd inherited.

At barrel six, however, I felt as if I'd been over-spritzed at Nordstrom's perfume counter. My senses were already overloaded. I couldn't smell; I couldn't taste. Proficient winemakers have almost an unlimited ability to avoid this sensory shutdown.

I drifted to a corner of the winery and relaxed with my ounce of remaining wine; it was almost time to call it a day anyway. Minutes later, Michael, our young cellarmaster, careened over to where I was sitting.

"Lose that wine," he said. "It's got crud in it."

I held the now-empty glass to the light and gritted my teeth.

"What kind of crud?"

"Bugs."

I didn't know if Michael meant bugs like earwigs or bugs like ebola, but that made little difference since they were already pirouetting in my digestive tract.

On one hand the incident was disheartening. I'd been enjoying that particular wine, feeling, in general, more competent about my tasting. Now this. Something in my glass was obviously foul, proving once again my ineptitude. On the other hand, Michael Stevenson, a very new friend, apparently cared whether I ingested bugs.

Later he showed me with the aid of a flashlight some maggot-like critters dangling on the inside of the bad barrel. My stomach threatened an uprising. That nearly empty barrel had been kicking around an obscure corner of the winery, untouched for years. The wine went down the drain and the bad barrel served out its remaining days as a deck planter.

To avoid mix-ups like the one I just described, we scribble a code on every barrel with white chalk. The annotation usually includes the vintage, the vineyard where the grapes were produced, the varietal, the section of the vineyard (this indirectly reveals the clone or genetics), and the tank where fermentation occurred. Here's a typical annotation on the head of a barrel: 2000, Shea, Pn, West Hill, 2A. Occasionally the name of an individual or a wine store is marked on the barrel as well. At our winery, that indicates the entire barrel has been purchased.

Despite the fact that similar barrels may contain wine from the same section—even the same row—of a vineyard, every barrel offers distinct flavor and aroma profiles. For this reason, all the barrel wine of a particular type—for instance, Shea Vineyard Pinot Noir—is combined in the metal tanks before bottling. Vintners strive for consistency so each bottle of a particular wine vintage tastes the same. If we bottled directly from the barrels, inconsistencies would be problematic.

To add to the confusion, all our French barrels arrive at the winery with another code already burned into their heads. Decipher this encryption and you decode the name of the cooper, the number of liters the barrel holds, the number of years the staves have been air-dried (if there's no symbol, it's typically two years), the town, and the forest where the oak was harvested. So a typical wood-burn code would read this way: Seguin Moreau, 228L, 3Y, Chagny, Bourgogne, Vosges. A+ refers to a medium-heavy toast. The cooper literally puts the barrel over a flame until the interior is charred to the desired level. When there is no plus sign, the barrel has undergone a medium toast. Buying barrels is not an easy task because so many variables are involved. Knowing the code is crucial for those working in the winery.

While in the barrels, the wine should pass through secondary or malolactic fermentation, the process by which sharp malic acid (as in a green apple) changes to softer lactic acid (as in milk).

Wine Notes:

MAKING SENSE OF MALOLACTIC FERMENTATION

After the initial (alcoholic) fermentation in the tanks in the days following harvest, Pinot Noir must still pass through a secondary fermentation in the barrel. Wines that have passed through malolactic are less biting, easier on the palate. While the initial fermentation is caused by yeast, malolactic fermentation is caused by bacteria and results in the transformation of malic acid to lactic acid. Lactic bacteria that cause the transformation are present in a winery's previously used barrels, even after the barrels have been cleaned. They jump from old barrels to new. If you put all new barrels in a new winery, however, the winemaker would have to inoculate the barrels the first year with lactic bacteria.

When we purchased Panther Creek, the building was not heated. The chemical process of malolactic fermentation depends on warm temperatures, so coaxing secondary fermentation was difficult. Thorough cleaning and sanitation practices assure that only the good bacteria influence the wine. Depending on variables such as the winery temperature and the amount of bacteria present, malolactic can begin within weeks of alcoholic fermentation, or, especially in unheated wineries, as late as the following spring when the building warms.

To speed malolactic fermentation and for human comfort, we heated our building as soon as we could. For secondary fermentation to occur, the wine must approach the sixty- to sixty-five-degree range.

A byproduct of malolactic fermentation, as with the initial alcoholic fermentation, is carbon dioxide. If the wine doesn't pass through the secondary fermentation and begins to "cook" in the bottle, it can explode from the internal pressure.

During the process of secondary fermentation, the winemaker slips special locks into the barrels' bung holes. These locks not only allow the gas to escape, but also allow winery employees to monitor the fermentation process. The opening in the lock passes completely through the bung. The water enclosed in the lock sputters like old-fashioned Christmas tree bubbler lights until malolactic fermentation is complete. Bubbling is created by the carbon dioxide in the barrel passing into the water in the lock.

If you happen to pull a cork on a "fizzy" Pinot Noir that wasn't meant to be a sparkler, the winery has made a mistake. (Some wines, on the other hand, are intentionally made this way; I especially enjoy some Italian Barberas that are referred to as *frizzante*, or slightly sparkling.)

One day Ron was upstairs in the office, figuring out if we'd ordered enough French oak barrels—at an astounding $700 each—to hold the wine we'd produced that first harvest; I was outside pruning the rose bushes that had been reaching out and snagging passersby. A curious man gripping a leash that tethered a small dog passed by me on the sidewalk. The dog sported a red bandanna. The man, obviously encumbered, lugged a bulging plastic grocery bag.

A drip of blood began somewhere on the man's scalp and trickled down his forehead between his eyes and dripped off the side of his nose. He couldn't wipe the blood from his face because his hands were full.

The man, who was probably about sixty, and the dog stopped short. Crouched in the bushes, I'd surprised them. Now I noticed sweat had popped up on the man's upper lip.

"Are you okay?" I asked.

"Not really," he answered.

I tried to imagine how he'd sustained a scalp wound. Could the pup have pulled the man into a post? Could a falling object have grazed his head? Already this seemed a bizarre situation, nothing like I'd encountered in my previous, apparently uneventful, life.

"Do you know your head is bleeding?" I asked. I was afraid if I approached, the dog might rip into me.

"I'm having a heart attack," he said.

I strained to make sense of his symptoms. "Then sit, sit on the sidewalk."

Slightly short of breath, he dropped the grocery bag and the leash and put his head in his hands. The dog broke free and dashed around in circles.

I'm leery of stray dogs even if they're small and look cordial. Quick little teeth do a lot of damage. I kept one eye on the terrier and one eye on the blood because the man had only accidentally swiped it.

I advised him to stay sitting on the sidewalk while I ran inside to summon an ambulance. At this news the man, let's call him Bert, began to sob—and begged me *not* to call the ambulance. My heart went out to him. I thought he must have been in crushing pain: chest, arm, jaw. Agitation is not advisable when someone is having a heart attack; I struggled to look calm and gather my wits.

"Okay, okay," I said soothingly. Where was that feed store employee who drove the forklift back and forth in front of the winery a thousand times a day? We were still commuting between Iowa and Oregon; I hadn't met most of the people in the neighborhood. Ron was far away at the back of the winery and up two flights of stairs. I needed help.

Just then Michael pulled up to the front of the winery. I couldn't believe my good luck.

"What's going on?" he asked as he jumped out of his Isuzu.

"This man's having a heart attack," I said pointing in the direction of the sidewalk, "but he doesn't want me to call for help." I was half panting; Bert was full-out crying.

Michael walked over and asked Bert a question or two. Bert wiped his eyes on his shirt sleeve.

Michael returned to where I was standing.

"He's shit-faced," Michael said.

The Oregon Liquor Control Commission (OLCC) stipulates that the inebriated are to be referred to as VIPs (Visibly Intoxicated Persons) by winery servers. Fortunately *we* hadn't served Bert.

Now the scene was making sense. This "presumed" shit-faced VIP had a blood-alcohol level that could easily have been associated with the drip down his forehead, not to mention the tears. Bert had, however, mentioned the heart attack thing.

"He's not having a heart attack," Michael said, reading my mind. "He just wants a ride the rest of the way home."

Why hadn't I picked up on this? I'd taken a full-day course put on by the OLCC on identifying drunks—excuse me, VIPs. I wondered if I'd ever be able to detect them. (And believe me, you're in trouble with the OLCC if you can't.) We'd learned VIPs laugh too enthusiastically, or not at all. They're too talkative, or too quiet. It's a ticklish call for a server when you've never laid eyes on the individual before he rambled into your winery.

Michael threw the man's groceries into the Isuzu, pushed the dog, still dragging its leash, into the backseat, and stuffed Bert, now looking woozy, into the front.

The hair on the back of my neck, my barometer of impending calamity, was prickling. Something wasn't right. "Do you know Bert?" I whispered at Michael.

"I've seen him around."

"Do you know where he lives?" I asked.

"No."

I was holding up progress. Bert, Michael, and the dog were ready to go.

"I'll follow you in my car," I said. My mind couldn't get around this situation. *Heart attack or no heart attack? VIP or no VIP? A VIP suffering a heart attack?* I was very uneasy.

We drove several blocks until Michael pulled to the curb in front of a small house in desperate need of a fresh paint job. I parked close behind. Bert tried to climb out of the Isuzu, but faltered. Michael and

I rushed toward him, and I could almost feel his little dog's teeth clamp into my ankle. But no, the terrier raced up the steps of the house and waited near the front door. I had to assume by the dog's exuberance we'd found the right place.

We half dragged Bert up the steps; I noticed the blood had begun to drip effusively with his exertion. Now the tiny stream had become a bloody river. We turned the knob, but the door was locked. I banged loudly on the screen, which shuddered in its frame.

Suddenly the door jolted open and two men, both looked like life-long members of an outlaw motorcycle club, raged onto the porch. (I admit, homemade tattoos intimidate me.) One of the men put his finger in my face and barked, "Get the hell out of here."

The other rowdy focused on Michael, who was seconds away from having his lights punched out. *I just knew something like this was going to happen.*

"Hey, we found Bert like this," Michael said.

"And he was already bleeding," I added. While one of the men was trying to push me off the porch, Bert clamped onto my forearm with both his hands and pulled me toward him.

"I want to thank you," Bert slobbered.

I swiveled, trying to avoid getting yanked in two. Then a very strange thing happened. I began to observe the scene in slow-mo as I might view a photograph: the rhododendrons lapping against the steps; the brilliant blue sky poking between the dark clouds; the gray paint peeling off the porch floor.

"Bert told us he was having a heart attack," I blurted as I came back to reality.

"Heart attack?" The hood hooted.

"Thanks so much," Bert repeated.

"Let go, please let go," I begged Bert, by far the weakest link.

The second hood had backed Michael out to the curb. Michael jumped in the Isuzu to avoid getting slugged and slammed the car door. Because of my gender and relative advanced age, I sensed I was going to survive this incident intact. Michael, however, looked to be a threat to Bert's gang and was in real danger. I heard Michael's car-door locks thunk. Seething at his missed opportunity, the rowdy gave up and walked back toward the house—toward me.

I pried Bert's fingers from my arm. "I hope you feel better," I said. In a rush of empathy, I wondered if Bert's housemates were kind to him. The hoodlum stalked through the doorway.

"Thanks so much," Bert repeated from inside, behind the screen. Without any more to-do the dog and I were suddenly old news standing out on the porch.

Michael and I drove back to the winery in our separate vehicles. Michael returned to work. I didn't want to interrupt him, but I also felt the need to review this situation. Nothing like this had ever happened to me in Iowa. The difference between Michael and me was that Michael already lived in McMinnville. He knew what and whom were normal and what and whom were abnormal, and the bottom line was, he didn't seem as perplexed as I felt. I had questions. Why was Bert bleeding? Would the thugs recognize us if we ran into them at the grocery store? What were they doing in that house? Would Bert get tanked again and come into the winery looking for another ride home?

Having memorized Bert's address, I made an impulse decision to call the police. "There's a guy in his sixties there who told me he was having a heart attack," I explained to the dispatcher. Actually, I hoped she'd read between the lines. There was more to this story, though I certainly didn't know what it was.

Michael passed by. "If you're talking about Bert, he really *wasn't* having a heart attack," he said.

Well, what else could I have said? I just thought some authority figure ought to investigate what was going on over there.

I tried to explain to Ron that I'd met a few of the new neighbors and been forced to call the police, but the story, as I told it, took its outlandish turns and Ron became lost in a quagmire of drunkenness, presumed hoodlums, and small dogs. The red spot on my arm where Bert had grabbed me faded too quickly to display as evidence.

Finally, frustrated, I said, "If you see a guy with a terrier wearing a bandanna, just don't get involved."

"I wouldn't," said Ron—wondering, I'm sure, if I'd finally cracked.

I hated to dwell on these minor challenges, although I couldn't help myself. Ron, too, was finding distress on the job. I realize now that in those anxious days we began to talk at each other rather than to each other—each expressing disparate concerns. For example, I carped about Bert's housemates and getting rejected at the wine festival as Ron rambled on about the price of barrels and the intricacies of labeling. Of course, Ron couldn't admit the depth of his worries because he'd made such an issue at the onset of this endeavor, going so far as to say in a quote in the newspaper that the winery was fulfilling a lifelong dream. I didn't have the heart to discharge the this-is-*your*-dream ammo because, on this same day, Ron discovered some of our winery expenses had become a nightmare. Figuring and refiguring, he was aghast at what his calculations showed. We'd been losing astounding amounts of wine through evaporation since the winery heaters had been installed. We lost five percent of Panther Creek's production (125 cases of wine) that first harvest through evaporation alone. Our wine was literally disappearing into thin air. The figure of five percent was easily calculated by the amount of topping wine we used to replace lost wine. Our winery angels were quite the tipplers and had to be reigned in, or we were going to go broke. Ron's next strategy was to install humidifiers to swell the barrel staves.

Although we'd planned to keep the moisture in the air at even higher levels, the old power plant "broke a sweat" above sixty-five to seventy percent humidity. When we pushed humidity levels higher than seventy percent, the barrel staves expanded to hold in the wine but condensation fogged the winery windows and "perspiration" dribbled down the brick walls. The temperature/humidity control was just another balancing act. Every time the humidity went out of whack, Ron, I noticed, left his office smelling slightly molded.

It was mid-November, just three months since Ron had bought Panther Creek. Our new vintage was barreled. We flew back to Iowa to a house devoid of daughters. The last of my garden flowers hung their brown heads and a layer of unraked leaves whirled about the lawn. Ron and I hadn't been alone at home for more than twenty years. At last I had to face the empty nest—and then pack it up for the move to McMinnville, which we'd scheduled for March. Though technically I was home, I can only describe my state of mind as homesick.

We were in constant contact with Mark, the Panther Creek wine-maker, who was also keeping track of the wine he'd made at St. Innocent Winery. Panther Creek and St. Innocent are separated by about twenty-five miles, a maze of curving highways, dairy farms, tree farms, koi farms, and the Willamette River. It's just too bad there's not a convenient bridge across that river somewhere between McMinnville and Salem, which is the state capital. Back and forth between the wineries several times each day, Mark was forced to rely on the ferry—a conveyance, in my opinion, for a past generation. The Wheatland ferry is tethered to a wire running perpendicular across the water so the boat and its six-car cargo won't drift sideways in the current and come ashore at a random landing downstream. At certain times of day the line of vehicles waiting for the ferry backs up adjacent to the riverbank. Smokers smoke, readers read, others watch the minute hand crawl around their watches. The sandy landing is located in a river bottom draped in hops vines and shaded with nut orchards, giving the area a gloomy other-world atmosphere even on sunny summer days. Once while Mark waited, an overloaded truck, angled precipitously as it boarded the ferry, dumped a load of fruit, making the plank too slick for other vehicles to board. That incident delayed our winemaker at least an hour in his exhausting schedule.

We wondered if Mark would—or physically could—stick with us. He'd been a vigorous forty when the crush began and looked sixty— ready for retirement, if not the retirement home—by the time Ron and I had left McMinnville. Mark's normally energetic speech had slowed to a slur like a recording set to the wrong speed; he hobbled with aches and pains resulting from overtaxed muscles and jammed joints; gray streaks showed in his beard. If we'd taken on more grapes, we might have killed him.

But fortunately Mark bounced back quickly; by Christmas he sounded like his old self, full of ideas for the next year. Yes—we'd been afraid to ask—he actually wanted to go through it again.

Calibrating probes are used to determine wine PH.

Laboratory measurements are vital during fermentation and bottling.

Westward Ho!

GAINST ALL ODDS, our house—the house where our children had grown up—sold in the depths of an Iowa winter. For once the ice and snow didn't bother me; I knew the spring thaw would signal the final good-bye to my friends and my Midwest family. My preoccupation was packing; I hadn't taken any writing jobs since harvest when we'd begun our trips back and forth to Oregon.

Once in awhile it occurred to me that perhaps I'd agreed to leave because I'd been left. My mother had died the previous summer with complications from Alzheimer's disease. Mom left us searching for her car in parking lots, overlooking holiday dinners, and finally forgetting our names. Our girls had gone to college, with the sounds of ripping packaging tape and snapping luggage locks. And of all things, my widowed dad—who had just missed sharing a golden wedding anniversary with my mother—had found himself . . . well, a girlfriend. They were planning to travel, he said.

Back in Oregon our first vintage was safely in the barrel, with some barrels still passing through malolactic fermentation. We heard the winery roof had sprung a leak or two, yet we saw no crucial reason to rush back to McMinnville until we made the move in March. Ginger, our real-estate agent, reported in regularly to say that the baloney house was leak-free and ready for move in.

Ron enlisted a network of distributors—the middlemen who sell wine between the winery and the retail outlets—by phone from Iowa as easily as he could have from his winery office in Oregon.

Wine Notes:

LATITUDINAL LOGIC

Move your finger in a straight line on a globe from Burgundy, France, around to North America. As your finger touches the western United States, where is it?

When we first came to Oregon, I heard repeatedly that the northern Willamette Valley was at the same latitude as Burgundy. Well, it's close. Panther Creek in McMinnville is located at 45 degrees, 12 minutes, 40 seconds North, latitudinally speaking. Beaune, France, epicenter of the Burgundy wine industry, registers 45 degrees, 43 minutes, 60 seconds North.

Why does this matter? It matters because Burgundy wine has long held the quality standard for Pinot Noir. These French wines are not only sought after, but they usually sport the highest price tags in the Pinot Noir industry. Naturally, Oregon vintners would like to cash in on the relationship between latitude and premium Pinot Noir.

Yet so many other factors come into play from vineyard (soil type and altitude, as examples) to winery (yeast and barrel selections) that it's difficult to single out latitude as the prevailing influence. We believe that the cool-climate viticulture in Burgundy and the Northern Willamette Valley can—with other factors cooperating—produce the zenith of Pinot Noir. Warm, sunny days and cool nights before harvest allow the flavors to rise in the fruit, creating nuances not found in hot climates where Pinot Noir must be picked early—when the fruit is ripe but flavors haven't had time to develop.

New World winemakers are finally giving the Burgundians a run for their money. American palates have begun to understand American Pinot Noir. The weak U.S. dollar, anti-French sentiment, high Burgundy prices, and an international wine glut haven't helped French winemakers in recent years. On the other hand, most vintages of French Burgundy, especially when aged, offer a plethora of delights. Little wonder Oregon winemakers, young Turks compared to their Franco counterparts, take note of our common latitude.

On the home front, frigid temperatures and ice storms pummeled the prairies, leaving extended hours for my packing. Understand, the term *packing* also encompasses trips to Goodwill, loads left at landfills and toxic waste drop-offs, and hundreds of trips to the top of the driveway dragging garbage bags. I was embarrassed by the mounds of paraphernalia we'd collected in nearly thirty years of marriage, including never-used wedding gifts, baby swings, Nintendo games, and a full collection of outgrown mittens and boots from size toddler to adult. I advertised a chilly garage sale and unloaded purses, stereos, porch furniture, and a chain saw I'd purchased in a panic after a tree toppled in our driveway several years earlier.

One of my oldest friends stopped by the day of the garage sale and shook her head. At least *I'd* come around to the idea that we were actually moving to Oregon.

"Why are you getting rid of this?" she said, grasping a vase. "I thought it belonged to your mother." I could tell she was angry; it's not easy to lose a friend—and we had been friends for two decades.

"That's true," I said, and moved the vase inside to the kitchen counter.

"I thought you had this bookcase in your bedroom when you were growing up," she commented.

We lugged the bookcase back into the family room.

I put the packing aside one afternoon to join Ron and one of his ex-law partners and his wife for lunch at a new Des Moines Italian restaurant. Of course, the conversation returned again and again to the subject of our impending move to Oregon. The woman said she'd be interested in hearing about my transition; she'd followed her husband in his pursuits, mostly international, several times. In fact, this friend said she was considering writing a book for the trailing wife. The term itself made me feel defensive. I didn't want to be thought of as *trailing*. I, after all, had a part in this decision and planned to take on responsibilities at the winery. Nevertheless, I inquired as to what she thought would make our move less trying.

One of her suggestions had been to pamper myself at first, focusing on getting plenty of rest.

"Take your time unpacking," she advised. "When you get to other places in the world, you'll find the Midwest's work ethic is overrated."

"And," she said, between spoonfuls of her Tuscan bean soup, "rest probably translates to napping."

Napping? I hoped the transition wouldn't be that trying. I wasn't, after all, suffering a life-threatening illness.

"Oh," she said, reading my thoughts. "You'll see, the stress will be powerful."

That's how it went with the move: two steps forward and one step back. I dropped off borrowed novels and ended up lingering three hours over a cup of coffee. I gathered several girlfriends and drowned my misgivings in the greasiest lunches possible: chili, tacos, grinders, burgers with extra fries. Following the chili bender, indigestion impeded my packing for several days. I lay on the sofa wallowing in dyspepsia and swigging Pepto Bismol; glued to Oprah, who seemed to have all the answers to life's problems, and Chef Caprial Pence's cooking program. I chose Caprial not for her culinary excellence or even because I wanted to think about food, but because her bistro is located in Portland. Eventually I rolled myself toward the boxes and tape. My final act of packing was digging out my grandmother's iris rhizomes for transplantation in my Oregon garden.

That last evening Ron and I ate a quiet, greaseless dinner with our neighbors, Jim and Gwen. I had become more aware of the wines I was served and tried to discern what characteristics I most enjoyed. To my recollection, we drank Panther Creek that night in celebration. I tried not to cry too much and left carrying a plate of Gwen's gooey brownies for the drive west. When we stepped outside, all four of us felt the vibrations of the moving van's idle gear through the soles of our shoes a half-block from the truck. The men were still loading. Through pure ignorance I'd booked the mother of all Mayflower vans, vast enough to haul two full households plus a small car to Oregon. In the dark its golden lights throbbed like a Tilt-a-Whirl. In fact, the running lights along the sides of the trailer illuminated the entire block. At least we were taking off in style; at least everyone knew we were leaving.

That night Ron and I squirmed in a creaky bed that was contracted to stay with the house. As the March sun rose the following day, I stripped off the sheets and stuffed them in a garbage bag that I carried with my suitcase to the car. I arranged my small, but well-loved, collection of orchid plants on the backseat.

We'd be on the road for four days, arriving with the moving van. Though we traveled in separate vehicles, I'm sure Ron was as choked up as I was, pulling away from our old lives. Our neighbors were still sleeping, newspapers lay untouched at the curb, shades were drawn when we passed by. I had a recurring thought of pioneer women walking the Oregon Trail, keeping pace with their wagons. I, probably like the pioneers, felt a rare mix of grief, eagerness, and fear. It was 6:30 A.M. I'd devoured two of Gwen's brownies before we hit the interstate a mile away. Ron said later that was about the time Chester the cat began to wail.

That first afternoon I followed Ron's new Land Cruiser into a rest stop somewhere in mid-Nebraska. Though the calendar read March, the temperature spiked freakishly to nearly eighty degrees. Ron and I lay on the brown grass in the picnic area and ate the rest of Gwen's brownies. For an hour we felt fat and happy and strangely liberated. Then we got back in our cars and turned onto Interstate 80, heading toward the sunset. Every so often I'd spot a reference to the overland trails and I'd wonder again how those heroic women had survived. About a half million immigrants traveled the Oregon Trail between the mid-nineteenth century and the beginning of the twentieth. The settlers swam their livestock through flooded rivers; I sped across bridges. They covered about fifteen miles a day; I hit speeds of seventy-five miles per hour. They cooked dwindling rations over a campfire; I dined heartily on restaurant fare. They slept under the stars with one eye open; I collapsed between fresh sheets. Why was *I* so wrung out?

Two days later we reached Wyoming, where the weather was as unseasonably cold as it had been unseasonably hot in Nebraska. My car shuddered in the wind as the highway breached vast expanses of flat pastures. The windshield wipers failed to keep pace with the sleet, then snow. Ron sped ahead, spurred by Chester's constant yowling, and I drove like a wimp afraid I'd end in a ditch tangled in barbed wire, listed among the missing like the Donner party. At noon when we stopped for an extended lunch at a diner where the men wore cowboy hats, my orchids gave up and froze in the backseat of the car. The wind was torture. I bet pioneers loathed that sound.

On the road again, I began to notice the growing size and number of trucks and feared getting sandwiched between them. Some were behemoth triple-bottom rigs; they flew at amazing speeds. The trucks looked like vehicles Mad Max would commandeer. Some were mud colored, laden with oily pots, pipes, gauges, and hoses. Others carted new Fords or logs, each log fatter and longer than a telephone pole. Occasionally sections of a double-wide trailer house whipped by me. Weigh stations, where the trucks had to exit, were my salvation. *Ha, ha,* I gloated. At least prairie schooners didn't have to share the path with semi-trailers.

Tumbleweeds rolled across the interstate and became snared beneath our cars' frames. We carried Wyoming tumbleweeds straight through to Utah. Ron arrived at our prearranged destinations sometimes as much as an hour before I did. I never listened to my CD's or tuned in the radio. I was reeling with thoughts about our new life in Oregon. Chester whined in Ron's ear all day and I, becoming more uptight over our hasty decision and certain bankruptcy, whined in his ear all night. With so many ways I'd envisioned to go wrong in the wine business, it was difficult for me to believe that there were just two turns in the entire eighteen hundred and fifty miles between Iowa and Oregon.

I would like to report that somewhere on the long haul west—perhaps on the shore of the Great Salt Lake, or even on the shoulder of I-84 near Pendleton or Baker City—I reached deep and pulled myself together. But that would be a flat-out lie. The adjustment, although it came, took longer for me.

Shea Vineyard has been the site of several "character-building" incidents.

CHAPTER 11

Just the Dirt

RON AND I had kept to our schedule; we'd bought the winery in late summer and now it was the following spring, exactly when we'd agreed to move to Oregon. We pulled into McMinnville—trailed by the Mayflower—at the time of year when Oregon soil erupts in a vegetal outburst that resembles a Jackson Pollock masterpiece with fields of red clover, streaks of yellow forsythia, splotches of green mint, and dribbles of purple pansies. In structured contrast, acres of grapevines mark fastidious rows along the dark hillsides. The tender buds emerge on the grapevines in April but stay hidden from roadside views until May. White blossoms follow in June.

The untamed grass at the back of winery—wild like the hair on a wakened child—had shot up, and Chester the cat couldn't get enough. He sniffed it, he slunk through it, he rolled in it, and finally, when he began to gnaw on it, we dragged the little beast inside where he keened by the door until we freed him again.

Oregonians should have a thousand words for green. Grass green, moss green, tender-leaf green, succulent green, conifer green, lichen green, algae green, kelp green, and ivy green. More greens to see than the imagination can conjure. While March may be a season of longing in most northern states, the month slaps Oregon with a wild green wallop.

Intrigued by plants I found in my new *Western Garden Book*, I struggled to memorize their exotic names: kangaroo paw, red hot poker, lily of the Nile, silk tree, passion flower. My home garden was virgin territory. My vaguely green thumb throbbed.

Despite Mother Nature's seduction, work was quite literally stacked up inside the baloney house. I felt especially low as the moving van pulled away, leaving me traversing a maze of corrugated boxes and crumpled packing paper. When the telephone rang, my heart leapt, particularly when I saw the Des Moines prefix on caller ID. I checked my watch. Perhaps it was Gwen.

I missed old friends, straight roads, vast horizons, and familiar shopping centers. I was out of my comfort zone in this valley between two mountain ranges. My thoughts were often in the flatlands where I recalled weeks of cloudless skies. Yet our Iowa home now belonged to another family. The week-old driver's license in my purse proved I was officially an Oregonian.

"I heard you moved to France," said the voice on the other end of the line. It was Honey, our ex-septic-tank repairman.

"But you dialed Oregon," I said. He must have heard something about a winery and assumed France.

"I was hoping you left my card with the folks who bought your house."

"Yes, I left a whole packet of stuff." *How depressing, my first call was from the septic-tank man.* And then, I reconsidered; Honey was, after all, a voice from my past. He'd done respectable work in a field most would sidestep.

"How's the weather there?" I asked.

"Flurries," he said. "But the ground has thawed." In the Midwest the thaw is especially remarkable for farmers, grave diggers, and septic-tank workers. Even office workers will tell you they notice the sensuous, earthy aromatics of softening fields that waft around on the first balmy days of spring. At a wine tasting we would term this bouquet *barnyard* and many individuals—not just Midwesterners like me—find the scent, as well as the flavor profile, most provocative.

"The ground never freezes in the Willamette Valley," I told Honey. "In fact, our neighbor's tulips are in bloom."

Hold on. Was I bragging about Oregon's climate? I couldn't believe those words had tripped over my tongue. On the other hand, this was spring as we always imagined it should be back in Iowa. Magnolias, plum trees, and chartreuse euphorbias were more than blooming; they were exploding, right in my new neighborhood.

My heart was lighter after hanging up with Honey, knowing they were still scraping windshields back in Iowa. It was difficult not to find solace in Oregon's brilliant palate of spring blooms.

The only cloud on my horizon was that every so often I worried about the wine festival debacle. Then, unexpectedly, my hackles were raised. "What the hell do they know?" I said, tearing into a pile of packing paper in my new McMinnville living room. I wouldn't subscribe to failure after we'd risked so much. The tasters' decision made me mad.

I was already aware of the subjectivity of wine tasting. Distinctive characteristics in the grapes make Shea Vineyard wine taste different from wine derived from, for example, Freedom Hill Vineyard grapes. Individuals often prefer one set of characteristics to another.

Soil type is one factor influencing flavor profiles. Oregon has dozens of soil types—Laurelwood, Jory, Cornelius, Willakenzie, Nekia, and Bellpine, to name a few. Apparently, even a Panther soil exists, though none of Panther Creek's fruit grows in it. Some of these soils allow for good water drainage; some are rich in organic matter, decayed plants, and animals; some offer a porous structure that allows for air circulation.

Jory soil is distinguished by its red color and slippery texture. My friend Martha Stewart (*not* the media maven), who with her husband John planted their vineyard more than a quarter century ago, tends her garden in tennis shoes that look as if they'd begun to rust. They call the area above Highway 99W between Lafayette and Dundee, Oregon, the Red Hills for a reason. Some soils, like Jory, are definitely better suited than others for viticulture (grape growing).

Soil is a component of terroir. *Terroir* is a term embracing all the conditions in a particular area of vineyard—from soil type to the direction of the prevailing winds, to the amount of annual rainfall. A wine's character, influenced by terroir, is described by color, mouth texture, aromatics (bouquet or nose), and taste (mouth). Wines are judged on these elements. And unlike any other food or beverage, wine is rated and ranked everywhere from intimate dinner parties to county fairs to *The New York Times*.

The whole idea of submitting our product for critical review was intimidating. The more I thought about it, the more the concept seemed ludicrous. Does Sara Lee send out her cheesecakes for commentary? Does the Green Giant send his Niblets to newspaper reviewers? Does Betty Crocker enter her angel food in cutthroat competitions? I don't think so.

"Why don't consumers just buy the wines *they* like?" I asked Ron. I'd become aware of men and women standing around reading the reviews (shelftalkers) stuck beneath bottles at the grocery store.

"I don't make the rules," he replied. "All I know is, it's important to participate in tastings and to send our wines in to the critics." He looked so beleaguered I decided to drop the subject. Temporarily.

Dan Dusschee, who owns Freedom Hill Vineyard with his wife, Helen, has been toiling in the vineyards for several decades. Their efforts have paid off with some of the most sought-after fruit in the state. Dan says Jory soils, as in the Stewart and Nysa vineyards northeast of

McMinnville, are made up of old, volcanic clay loam. Think about nearby Mount St. Helens, still a hotbed of underground activity, and that's no surprise. Volcanic explosions resulting in mudflows and ash have occurred for millions of years around the Willamette Valley.

The Bellpine-type soil at Freedom Hill Vineyard is the oldest soil in the northern Willamette Valley. It's a silty, clay loam emerging from marine sediment. The older the soil, the more time the nonorganic elements, such as minerals, have had to break down. If you believe the French, dissolved rather than solid minerals are easier for the vines to absorb.

Willakenzie soil, as in the Shea and Bednarik vineyards, is alluvial, like a river bottom. Tons and tons of Oregon soil arrived special delivery from Montana during the Missoula floods at the time of the Ice Age. In several momentous torrents when ice dams in a glacial lake gave way, walls of water bolstered with boulders the size of condominiums barreled westward through the Columbia Gorge and thundered onto the Willamette Valley floor. A lot of Montana in the way of clay and silt, characteristic of alluvial soils, was displaced into Oregon during the Missoula Floods. If Hollywood ever makes a movie on location in an Oregon vineyard, I think scene one should open with the arrival of the Willakenzie soil.

Even experts have difficulty attributing particular characteristics, such as Freedom Hill's typical black-cherry bouquet, to a single aspect of terroir, although I think I can offer an extreme example of "something in the soil." Ron and I spent several weeks traveling through France with our daughters during the summer my older daughter graduated from high school. This road trip transpired four years before we bought Panther Creek. We'd been traveling for several weeks when we lit on the inviting, Provençal burg of Chateau Arnoux. As I think back, the main street could have come directly from the movie *Chocolat*. Most charming.

The villagers were celebrating what we theorized was an annual festival highlighted by a carnival and fireworks extravaganza. At dusk the celebration peaked with the discharge of torpedo-like bombs from the shell of a dilapidated building. I'll never forget the "fun-loving" firemen who showered live sparks the size of Ping-Pong balls on the crowd, as well as the wine Ron and I shared soon after to calm our frazzled nerves. The wine was less exciting than the sparks, but as remarkable.

It was a Bandol, local, and suggested by our waiter. Bandols tend to be big, red wines that incorporate the Mourvèdre grape. Our first swallows revealed the bouquet: olives, powerful olives, a liquid tapenade. And not to our liking. Even with my uneducated palate, I was revolted by the staggering essence of olives.

In that particular area of France, the vineyard where those wine grapes were grown probably had a history as an olive orchard. Or perhaps the olive trees grow adjacent to the Mourvèdre vineyard. One way or another, the olive flavor leached into the soil and worked its way into the wine grapes. I've never been certain if the residents of Chateau Arnoux enjoy the flavor of olives in their wine, or if the waiter assumed we wouldn't notice.

Far from France in Waterloo, Iowa, where Ron and I grew up, all roads lead to farm fields. My father used to tell me the richest soil in the United States, if not the world, blanketed our county. I don't know whether agronomists agree with Dad, but I do know Black Hawk County is corn country, and corn thrives in black, fertile, organically rich soil. Generally the darker the soil, the higher its organic nutrients. In the prehistoric era before television, my parents entertained us by taking country drives. It was not unusual for my dad, a native Iowa farm boy, to coast our Chevy wagon (yes, I had four younger sibs) along the shoulder of a gravel road to let us embrace those long, flat stretches of tilled blackness.

Once, decades ago, I was folded in the backseat between the sibs and a small band of my mother's relatives, exotic visitors from the faraway East Coast, when we swerved off the road. An overnight case bumped between my knees. I held someone's pillow on my lap.

"Do they burn the fields to get the ground so black?" the cousin asked. Fresh off the plane and she was already snared in my father's sticky web. Little did she know the subject of black dirt could be as infinite as the Iowa horizon. A historical discourse followed, beginning with the crops first cultivated by the Plains Indians. In other words, dinner was late that night.

Growing up, we marveled at May's first bristle of corn shoots and August's forest of stalks. Today those prime, fertile fields sell for about $2,500 an acre. Very few Iowa farmers relinquish corn to grape production, although the aspect of a perennial crop is apparently attractive to some. Oregon, ranked second in number of wineries in the United States next to California, has more than five hundred vineyards compared to Iowa's thirty. The climates allow for very different varietals. For example, Iowa grape growers who cultivate red varieties like Concord and Maréchal Foch in their environment of extremes would be daredevils to plant finicky Pinot Noir. Iowa farm soil looks like dark, rich Godiva. Oregon's vineyard soil often appears more like Russell Stover.

In this case, the Russell Stover is much more costly. Bare unimproved vineyard property in the northern Willamette Valley goes for between $10,000 and $20,000 an acre, depending on factors such as elevation (best for Pinot Noir, between 250 and 750 feet) and orientation (south, southeast, or southwest).

Furthermore, premium Pinot Noir grapes turn up their noses at fertile soils. The vines' struggle creates character in the wine in much the same way that human struggle endows character—or so they claim.

Struggle is not necessary for all wine grapes, but with Pinot Noir, low fruit yields allow for more powerful flavors. The best flavors and structural qualities become concentrated in a few grapes rather than being spread—and diluted—through many.

In April, a few weeks after our official move to Oregon, Dick Shea, owner of Shea Vineyard, Michael, Ron, and I set out on a mission to check out Panther Creek's parcel of Pinot Noir in Dick's vineyard. As the Land Cruiser dropped into low gear, adjusting to the steep rise up from the highway to the vineyard, we couldn't have guessed we were in for one of those character-building incidents.

At last, row after fastidious row after fastidious row of woody vines pruned to wire trellises on one hundred fifty hillside acres fanned before us. The sight was even more glorious than photographs I'd pored over in coffeetable books.

We parked near the gate, which was locked to exclude vandals as well as legitimate visitors who might inadvertently be carrying phylloxera on their shoes or clothing. Phylloxera is an unwelcome insect that kills grape stock by nibbling their roots. We waited near the gate, caught up in the vineyard scene, as Dick searched for his key.

Wine Notes:

THE PHYLLOXERA BLIGHT

People often ask if any of our vineyard parcels have suffered phylloxera damage. The quick answer is yes.

Phylloxera is a disease caused by an aphid that nibbled at the roots of France's grapevines in the mid-1800s, which devastated the industry and, on a more personal note, the morale of grape growers and wine lovers around the world. The blight flew through Europe. In time, phylloxera infected European hybrids planted here in the United States. California was hard hit.

Interestingly, native American grapevines are impervious to the insect's damage. In fact, it is generally thought that the importation of native American grapevines to Europe introduced phylloxera there. Phylloxera travels on cuttings, roots, tools, boots, and even car tires.

You may wonder why American vineyard owners didn't plant resistant native American grapevines. The answer has to do with the flavor of the wines produced by these grapes. *Vitis vinifera*, the European species, is thought by many consumers to result in a higher-quality product. Native American grapes can produce wines that are said to taste "foxy"—and if you think foxy is a compliment, guess again. In this case, foxy translates to damp-fur flavors and aromas. While barnyard flavors can be positive, foxy usually ranks on the p.u. scale.

Oregon vineyards, including some Panther Creek leases, are now affected by phylloxera. Eventually, all Panther Creek's vineyard sections planted with old *Vitis vinifera* vines will probably succumb.

Phylloxera was so slow to invade Oregon that the state's wine pioneers didn't plant resistant root stock, thinking the scourge would never hit here. Maybe, for instance, the climate was too cool. When Ron and I first came to wine country, the vineyards where we do business had not suffered problems. Vigilant visitors tripped through shoe baths before traveling from one vineyard to another. Yet Dan Dusschee explains that phylloxera clings to pant cuffs, as well as the fur of the vineyard dog or the legs of trespassing deer. The aphid was impossible to restrain once it was introduced, and Oregon vineyards now show phylloxera damage. Aerial infrared photography often depicts the earliest signs.

Vineyard managers are currently replanting old vines that show early color changes, and later wilting, with *Vitis vinifera* vines grafted to resistant native American grape root stock. (The root stock portion of the plant does not transmit the foxiness.) The disease is as devastating to Oregon farmers as it was to Europeans more than a century ago. Yet, knowledge is power—and planning for the worst eases the negative economic impact. Fortunately entire vineyards are not wiped out in a single year, so parcels are being replaced on an annual basis.

Back in the vineyard, Dick Shea turned his pockets inside out. "I don't have it," he said at last, returning to the car for a second look.

No key.

We examined the fence and located a place where it was just possible to scramble through. We could leave the car and walk to the Panther Creek parcel ten minutes up the hill.

No key, no problem. I was, after all, an Iowa girl who'd spent her childhood crawling through fences.

The sunlight filtered through the clouds—intensifying colors and making the buds, which had broken through the vines, an unnaturally vibrant green that contrasted with the dark earth. I took a deep breath of fresh-from-the-sea air tinged with aromas of blossoms, new leaves, and turned soil.

We trekked to the Panther Creek parcel, awed by the fertile hollow of the Willamette Valley bordered by the rugged Coast Range to the west. We pointed out landmarks and beauty spots on other hills, such as an apple orchard whose white flowers brushed the blue-black clouds that shifted above them.

Examining the grapevines with our hands, we could feel new life pushing outward. Spring precipitates a mingling of eagerness and impatience in vineyard and winery people. The buds always seem slow to burst through the vines—and then when they do appear, they unfurl their small green flags in snail time. That day, weather fronts gyrated above our heads, but we were oblivious.

Ron, Michael, and Dick, wary of mildew in the coming season, discussed what they hoped would be appropriate combative measures. I listened, thinking just nine months earlier, Ron was at his law office writing construction contracts, rather than on a hillside in Oregon discussing the prevention of mildew and phylloxera. Both of us had hit the ground running; I just had farther to go.

I ambled down the path for a view of the careening hills to the north of the vineyard. Taking in yet another broad, grass-green vista, I was snared by the excitement of springtime in the vineyard. The beginning of a new vintage—and for us, a new life.

I didn't have long to ruminate on those feelings because at that moment, the clouds dumped so much rain, it was as if I were standing in a car wash rather than in a vineyard. Rain hammered down on me, drenching my clothes, slathering my skin, matting my hair.

With the guys in the lead, we took off sprinting; but when we reached the bottom of the hill, out of breath and dripping, the gate was, naturally, still locked. For unknown reasons the fence was all but impossible to navigate from the other direction. Two shivering people struggled to separate the wires for the hapless individual contorting through. We were as breathless from the icy cold as we were from the run. There was no talking, just the chattering of teeth, during the drive back to the winery.

Yet just as quickly as a storm can drift over a mountain range, things began to pick up (for me). Later that same week I drove to the neighborhood grocery store for a few items I needed for a dinner party. A portion of a vintner's work—and it's admittedly a stretch to call this work—is entertaining with food and wine. I'd honed several tasty recipes that could be whipped up with confidence and, more important to me, speed. One of those recipes fulfilling both requirements is a fish dish for which I mash potatoes; sauté chopped, red chard (or bok choy) in a little olive oil; and bake halibut fillets with dill, lemon, and butter. I stack each of the three ingredients on a dinner plate—mashed potatoes, chard, and halibut—then embellish with a side of colorful relish. *Voilà!* Dinner is served.

I was checking out the halibut when I spotted two sketchy guys, *my God, Bert's housemates*, sauntering toward me. They were donned in the same attire as when last we met: studded leather boots, filthy jeans, and open shirts with flapping tails. In a defensive maneuver, I ducked my head and perused the vast variety of frozen products, finally feigning interest in the back panel of a carton of Gorton's Fish Sticks.

The tattooed ones came so near I could smell the cigarette smoke clinging to their clothes and see the dirt caked under their fingernails. My pulse thudded in my forehead. My fingers quivered on the fish sticks.

The men gave me a laggard once-over, resolved I was just another middle-aged matron, and then separated widely, allowing me to pass. My anxiety was for naught.

I couldn't have asked for a more favorable response; I didn't ring a bell (if there was a bell to ring) with these two. The only remains of that day are a frozen box of fish sticks buried somewhere in my freezer.

Some comforting words for a newcomer like me came from soft-spoken David Bergen. David and his wife own Tina's Bistro located just east of McMinnville in the burg of Dundee. It's a rare evening a Willamette Valley vintner or winemaker isn't on the premises dining on steaming scallops and cobblers worth the calories.

"How are you adjusting?" David asked me a few weeks after the Mayflower had deposited our earthly belongings at the baloney house. We were dining at the restaurant with B&B owners, Doris and Lynn Steiger.

"Mostly okay," I admitted.

"You'll land on your feet. We're all immigrants here," David said. He had grown up on the East Coast. I was beginning to find solace in successful relocation stories. Doris hailed from Colorado—and she'd not only survived, but was prepared to move again. Several of our McMinnville neighbors had relocated from California. I'd already hooked up with two walking pals, both new arrivals, one from Idaho, the other from Pennsylvania. David was right; I was beginning to feel slightly less like an emigrant and more like an immigrant. A fine but important distinction.

Leaves and fruit flourish during Oregon's sunny summer months.

CHAPTER 12

Testing the Terroir

URING THOSE FIRST months living in Oregon, I noticed that
Northwesterners revealed startling dissimilarities from the
Midwesterners we'd known. While Iowans seemed to bow at the
altar of the work ethic, I found Oregonians more likely to revere
courage—as in the courage to change. To my delight, Ron and I had
achieved a certain distinction just by uprooting ourselves from our old
lives. Our new acquaintances were intrigued with our story. What
brought us to Oregon? What had we left behind? I think they found us
interesting because so many Oregonians, a transient breed, have accomplished long-distance moves themselves—so they're sympathetic
to the sacrifices and difficulties that arise from relocation. They know
the trauma of being yanked from familiar terroir and then trans-
planted in foreign soil.

I enrolled in a short course held at the McMinnville library offering to provide me with an understanding of the West and its citizens.
The fact the course was even offered speaks to the numbers of disori-
ented newcomers. One lecturer speculated about the cast of unusual
characters who speckle the Left Coast. He relayed the old joke that
God was so ecstatic after forging the glorious Northwest, he moved the
continent to eye level for a closer inspection. In doing so, the creation
teetered, thus causing all the nuts to roll toward the West Coast.

The more academic argument purports the theory that the Wide Open Spaces have always lured folks who chafed at the confines of life in traditional society. Yet, the lecturer explained, sometimes these "misfits" have been harbingers of the most imaginative endeavors. Think Hollywood. Think about all of those who followed a dream.

I secretly worried that Ron and I fell into the misfit category. My ninety-three-year-old grandmother confided that my grandfather, yearning for a walnut orchard, had urged her to leave Iowa and move to Oregon with him when they were young, back in the 1930s. She said it was one of the few times, with the weight of three little children hanging on her apron strings, she'd put *her* foot down.

We'd lived in the baloney house for just a few weeks when I discovered myself napping voraciously. I rose with Ron at seven, and when he went downstairs about eight, I dragged along in my pj's and watched him eat his oatmeal. As soon as Ron's car left the driveway, I'd pass out again on the family-room sofa.

Waking several times each morning and gaping at my watch, I'd vow, guiltily, to pull myself upstairs, take a shower, and get dressed by 9:00 A.M., then 10:00; 10:30 for sure. I felt that queasy exhaustion I'd only known in the early months of my pregnancies—several decades earlier.

Sleep was most seductive on the dreary days, of course. Rain pummeled our roof and rumbled in our downspouts; fog pushed like a gray blanket against the windows. I was out.

Dismissing an unexpected pregnancy at age forty-nine, I next considered stress and depression. I thought back to our old friend's words at the Italian restaurant. Hadn't she mentioned napping by the *trailing* wife? So far her Midwest work-ethic theory held water. Maybe she was right about the stress of moving too. I'd been warned, though I thought I was feeling very little tension.

In all honesty, however, I was a little down about the house. Neighbors, admitting to self-guided tours during its construction, trilled on about how much they admired it. They mentioned the built-ins in the master bedroom and the ceramic tile in the master bath.

Several of our wine acquaintances said they were taken with the high-tech appliances and generous cabinetry in the kitchen. Entertaining, they pointed out, is critical in the winery business.

I told my new friend, Helen Dusschee, who owned Freedom Hill Vineyards with her husband Dan, that I didn't like the place. "What style would you call it?" I asked.

She shrugged. "New?"

"You see, it has no style." I was still wishing for a Colonial or a Tudor.

Helen looked around and shook her head. "I hear what you're saying," she sighed, "but you're not going to find a little brick house here in Yamhill County." Helen hailed from Ohio, so she understood what I was missing.

I happened on a romantic farmhouse skirted by a sweet-smelling clover field. I drove Doris there and pulled my car up close to the fence so we could take in the full scene. Mares nuzzled their colts by the fence.

"I like this," I told her.

"But it's tainted," she replied in that matter-of-fact way she announced the breakfast menu back at the B&B.

"Tainted?"

"Someone was murdered here."

I sped back to the highway. Lewis and Clark had Sacajawea; I had Doris to guide me through alien territory. My house was looking better.

Things certainly weren't bad enough for me to be sleeping my days away. In fact, once out of the house and exploring, my weariness evaporated into a new sense of freedom. I had shed the deadlines and obligations that seemed to expand geometrically through the years as we'd furrowed in with our family. I'd attended my last parent-teacher conference and high school soccer game. I had no pressing deadlines. My responsibilities at the winery in the nonharvest months were limited and pleasurable. Basically I was unencumbered. So, what was wrong? I'd begun to think I was under the influence of another psychosomatic condition, at least while I was in the house. My sneezing and itching had been replaced by a baffling sleeping sickness. I didn't have a doctor in McMinnville—and I was too wiped out to find one.

The mystery was solved, not coincidentally, after Ron purchased some new patio equipment a few weeks after we'd moved into the baloney house. Somehow, our old grill hadn't made the Mayflower. It was still spring and Ron was eager to fire up the barbecue.

We spent an impatient hour assembling, counting screws, and piecing the unit together from hood to wheels. I carried out the burgers from the kitchen just as Ron flipped on the gas.

"What is that wretched smell?" I asked.

"Just a little propane." Ron fiddled with the valve.

Another whiff and I knew. I'd asked several people if they noticed a sweet, sickly scent in the family room.

"It's that new-house smell," they'd said, putting their noses in the air and snuffing loudly. When Ron, a lover of fresh air, came home in the evenings, he'd inevitably thrown open the windows. Yet because mornings in the Willamette Valley are chilly, I'd close up as soon as his car pulled out of the garage. Escaped propane from fireplaces in the closed-up family and living rooms had been sickening me. My terroir had been poisoned, and I wasn't a bit happy.

"This house hates me more than I hate it," I sniped. Ron pretended not to hear.

As soon as a plumber sealed the joints in the leaking fireplace-propane lines, my problems vanished. I wasn't quite ready to give up on my grudge, however.

"I don't think any real damage was done," Ron said.

"Because you're at the winery all the time, you haven't noticed." Our dinner was sitting in front of us, growing cold.

"Then go to a doctor and see what she says."

"That would probably mean a battery of miserable tests."

"Suit yourself." He put his napkin on his lap. "You seem the same as before."

"What's that supposed to mean?"

"Has someone told you you're having problems?"

"I didn't know these people before. They probably assume I've always been this way."

My dad had suffered a series of small strokes and the doctors asked him to recite the names of the presidents, backwards, to check for permanent damage.

"Clinton, Bush, Reagan," I began.

"See, nothing's wrong." Ron picked up his fork.

"I'm stuck. I'm already stuck. Oh, Carter."

"Allison was born during the Ford administration."

"Emily was born during Nixon's term."

"There's nothing wrong with your brain. You're going to be okay. Honest."

I decided there was a chance Ron was right. I was happy to know I wasn't psychosomatic, depressed, or permanently damaged; but, as you know by now, I'm not a person who suffers discomfort without complaint.

PALM TREES, IN MANHATTAN?

Unlike me, Pinot Noir grapes are masochists. Pinot Noir thrives in winter rain and summer drought. Their roots burrow into recesses where corn or soybeans would die of thirst. Not all grape varieties will suffer through similar growing conditions. For instance, Cabs like it hot. You don't find

Cabernet growing on Willamette Valley hillsides for the same reason you don't find palm trees shading the avenues of Manhattan. The conditions aren't right.

When customers ask us why Panther Creek doesn't produce one of their favorites—a Cabernet or a great Grenache—we have to say we can't. Or, I should say, the northern Willamette Valley can't produce the grapes without major headaches. You'll want to travel to France, Spain, California, or Washington to visit wineries producing those specialties.

Much Willamette Valley vineyard property is ideal for Pinot Noir and, of course, a limited variety of other fine wines. As I mentioned before, terroir is a term embracing all vineyard conditions—from soil type to the direction of the prevailing winds, amount of annual rainfall, average daytime temperatures, etc. Terroir varies from one section of a vineyard to another. Occasionally during harvest, some rows of a vineyard ripen and the fruit gets picked as much as a week before similar fruit growing just a few yards away.

At Nysa Vineyard in the Red Hills, the owner, a scientist, divides each row of grapes among his three winery customers. That way no winery gets dramatically different grapes from the other two. This process, I might add, makes farming much more difficult because each third of a row is farmed differently, according to the vintner's wishes. This grower is meticulous in his quest for evenhandedness.

Unbelievably, Shea Vineyard soon became the site of yet another character-building opportunity (remember the soaked-to-the-skin incident?). This time the problem was also terroir-induced. Our Iowa neighbors, Jim and Gwen, had flown to Oregon for a short visit. While Gwen and I shopped in Portland, the guys opted for a vineyard tour. The day was unseasonably cool and unreasonably rainy. Late in the afternoon Gwen and I dodged rush-hour traffic in a downpour, returning home with our purchases to discover the guys were still out touring. Dusk fell and our dinner reservations at Nick's Italian Café in McMinnville loomed.

"There's a problem," reported my older daughter Emily, who was home on a short respite from graduate school. Gwen and I had heard those words many times during our children's teen years. "There's a problem," they said when their orthodontist reported they'd be wearing braces for another two years. "There's a problem," they said when a classmate creamed their Honda in the school parking lot. "There's a problem," they said when I assumed they'd return home from the prom at midnight and the kids had planned for sunrise. I feared those words. This time Emily was clutching the telephone receiver, and I couldn't fathom what revelation was to follow.

"Dad and Jim are stuck up in Shea Vineyard," she said.

I imagined mud flying, wheels spinning, axles grinding. I imagined loud cursing. Shea Vineyard is located in the heart of the Oregon countryside, miles from any town.

Em continued, "I called a wrecker."

Really? "But how could you tell the tow-truck driver where to go?" I asked. Emily, who spent most of her time at the University of Washington, had never set foot in Shea Vineyard.

"Dad tried to give me the directions on his cell phone," she said. Gwen drew a quick breath at the word *tried*.

"But," she continued, "it was hard to hear. He had to walk to the top of the vineyard to get reception." Outside the rain was drifting in sheets. I imagined more cursing.

No straight shot exists between McMinnville and the vineyard. The highway stops, starts, and swoops around and through fields and hillsides. Moreover, Shea Vineyard doesn't have a sign. A person just has to be familiar with the highway turnoff.

"Oh, boy," I said. "Did the tow guy sound like he knew where he was going?"

"He said he had an idea," Em said.

Only an idea? Ron and Jim were fellow fishermen; but away from the lake, they were not renowned for their prowess in the wilderness. I looked through the window and noticed (*could it be?*) sleet had commingled with the rain. At least, I thought, the guys would stay dry in the car. I imagined they were hungry; our usual dinner hour had already come and gone. If the tow truck couldn't pull the Land Cruiser out, I assumed the driver would at least bring the guys back to McMinnville. The biggest assumption of all was that the tow-truck driver would stumble on the vineyard. Fortunately, Ron had the cell phone.

After an hour of staring at the door, Gwen and I decided to get some nourishment at Nick's, just blocks from our house, in the event we had to forge a trail to the middle of nowhere in a cloudburst—in the dark. We could be reached by phone at the restaurant as easily as we could be reached at home.

We were halfway through Nick's minestrone when the guys appeared, looking drained and faintly blue. Globs of mud clung to their shoes. Ron's waxed coat dripped water; his fingers were pruned. Their ordeal was more disconcerting than we'd imagined.

Apparently Ron had parked the Land Cruiser on a hillside road in order to point out Panther Creek's section of grapevines. Suddenly the vehicle, with Jim and Ron still inside, began to slide sideways, picking up speed as it skittered down the embankment. Of course, pumping the brakes proved useless.

If it weren't for Dick Shea's trellising (the structures that support the grapes), the guys might still be sliding. Or, worse, rolling. The vineyard plunge and subsequent crash was jolting to Ron's psyche, though damage to the SUV and property was minimal. Who would have guessed Oregon's Willakenzie mud could be as slick as Iowa ice? I pushed my wineglass toward Ron and ordered two more bowls of minestrone, ASAP.

Ecosystem is a capricious concept in Oregon, in and out of the vineyard. Rain can be falling at my house while several blocks away an errant wind whirls dust in the schoolyard.

One of our McMinnville neighbors, making the most of our climatological conditions, planted her front yard with cacti, which are marginal plants for the soggy Northwest. Most cacti prefer a hot dry climate, sandy loam, and sun. Surprisingly, the prickly plants survived in her protected terroir; some even flourished. Palm trees grow too. I wouldn't say they're abundant, but they grow in Oregon. I've marveled at a 1920s-era postcard picture of a massive cedar stump that housed a family of five. Cedars, sequoias, Douglas firs, and redwoods thrive here. The mighty beams that span the winery building ceiling were fashioned from old-growth fir.

As May drizzled on, I became more and more flabbergasted at the size and color of my garden blooms. Our home garden terroir proved extraordinary. My grandmother's irises, which had traveled as rhizomes wrapped in newspapers on the backseat of my car, had never grown taller; each stem struggled to lift a purple-black bloom the size of my shoe. My daisies were waist high.

Smiling at a wanton intermingling of lavender, pink, and orange azaleas in a yard along Highway 99, I hated to admit that my days of nursery exploration had produced a similar indulgent display. For starters, I'd purchased a topiary lilac. A weeping cedar. Three crab-apple trees. Eighteen rose bushes of different varieties. Several hot-pink fuchsia baskets. Orange nasturtiums for salads. Golden yarrow for tea. An artichoke for its bizarre flowers. Nothing died; every plant, every bush, every cutting took hold. The terroir was just too tempting.

As far as I know, there is no Gardeners' Anonymous—although many suffer from the over-planting syndrome. Drive down any street and you can point out its victims. I know a family who avoids their front door because an anonymous someone planted a giant redwood too near the house.

One afternoon after stealthily planting a dozen hostas before Ron returned from the winery, I came on a small article in the McMinn-ville *News Register* concerning a Master Gardener class with a few openings. So, there was help for people like me. Could I commit to a weekly meeting? For the sake of my garden as well as my pocketbook, I had no choice.

The class was a mix of novices and semi-pros, but we all had an equal shot at success thanks to the comprehensive manuals. The subject matter ranged from slugs to soil amendments to grapevine pruning. My new friend, Martha Stewart, already a gardener extraordinaire and vineyard owner, had also signed up.

I learned as much about people as plants in the course. We hailed from all walks of life: rich and poor, farmer and urbanite, college educated and street smart. Yet I discovered through our first conversations that anyone who takes time to nurture a seedling is probably willing to nurture human relationships as well. I also discovered that there are Master Gardeners and there are *Master Gardeners*! I'd been smug about my competence with Midwest plants: roses, geraniums, petunias. But the Willamette Valley's growing season of 280 days allows for those mundane specimens, as well as exotics such as bamboo, fan palms, and the astounding monkey puzzle tree, whose leaves resemble an origami project. Fortunately for me, the Master Gardener test is open book—and even then I was forced to use the phone-a-friend option for a fertilizer equation. At least by then, I had a friend to phone. In fact, I made several friends in the class.

One morning during a lecture on tree trimming (never top a tree), an animated young woman passed me a folded paper. When I opened it, I discovered detailed instructions for producing massive quantities of, what appeared to be, *a love potion*. The elixir involved an aged barrel of Pinot Noir fortified with herbal additives. I raised my eyebrows. Could this be the romance in winemaking I'd sought?

"It's spring and the sap is rising," my classmate whispered.

Ron was one hundred percent *not* interested, though he sensed Alcohol, Tobacco and Firearms, who oversee and enforce U.S. wine production, would be drawn to the concoction—and not in a positive way.

One of the reasons ATF takes such an interest in wine production might be in response to a wine imported into the United States from France in the late 1800s. They called the *tonique* Vin Mariani; the wildly popular wine's secret "therapeutic" ingredient apparently turned out to be cocaine. Importers couldn't get enough—until Vin Mariani was jerked off the market. When the ATF enters Panther Creek to check our production against our grape purchases and the alcoholic content of the wines, the officers are armed. The visits are unscheduled and supersede any other winery activity.

Ron handed back my new friend's love potion recipe. "I think this could be poisonous," he said.

I rolled my eyes. For once he was wrong; but the word *poisonous* terminated that conversation. I did agree that we had our hands full making regular wines.

While the encounter with Bert's friends ended positively, Ron and Jim survived their adventure in the vineyard, and I was liking the way my garden enhanced the appearance of the baloney house, the rejection from the Pinot Noir celebration still weighed heavily. Whenever I asked Ron what we could do, he'd say, "Forget it."

The rejection was difficult to disregard when conversations in the wine community turned again and again to the upcoming gala event. All our other vintner friends had made the cut.

Fog is a frequent visitor to valley vineyards.

CHAPTER 13

The Open House

OTHER SEASONS in the winery don't offer the exhilaration of the harvest months, though the calm times are welcome to crush-weary workers. Visitors, however, continued to stream year-round into Panther Creek for barrel tastings and the opportunity to learn more about the mysteries of winemaking, which we were just ferreting out for ourselves.

Most Yamhill County wineries open to the public Memorial Day and Thanksgiving weekends. Even wineries without full-fledged tasting rooms like Panther Creek take part in the popular three-day events. Highway 99W bogs down with traffic between Portland and McMinnville and area restaurants are clobbered with the overwhelming press of reservations.

A vague apprehension about the upcoming Memorial Day open house gnawed at the backs of our minds that first spring as Ron and I literally wandered farther and farther afield, acquainting ourselves with newfound seascapes and mountain paths.

Martha and John Stewart had become our hiking pals. One fog-gripped Saturday our new friends demonstrated to Ron and me how to edge along the slippery rocks *behind* one of the crashing waterfalls at Silver Falls State Park. The park is nestled in the foothills of the Cascade mountain range—southeast of McMinnville, beyond the hillside vineyards, tulip fields, hazelnut orchards, and grass-seed farms. Besides the Stewarts, I put faith in my new hiking boots as I found my footing and gazed through the waterfall's mist toward the green gorge beneath us. I couldn't tell if my heart was fluttering from balancing on the cusp of the narrow trail or from the beauty beyond. Above, the lofty firs, some more than two hundred feet high, left us feeling as diminutive as a line of ants.

John and Martha rank among Oregon's first wave of winegrape growers. They didn't trellis their vines on wires as other vineyard owners did. Their vines were head trained; when trimmed, each looks like an oversized, top-heavy topiary.

Ron and I purchased Pinot Noir and an unusual white grape called Melon from Martha and John. The Melon (put the accent on the second syllable) enjoys a staunch following because of the way it pairs with seafood, especially shellfish. In France, Melon is called Melon de Bourgogne, or Muscadet.

When they purchased the Melon starts, the Stewarts were told the vines were Pinot Blanc. Melon is difficult to grow in the cool-climate Northern Willamette Valley terroir; Pinot Blanc had proved more trustworthy. But the Melon thrived in the Stewarts' terroir, and customers began to crave the fleeting exotic flavor the wine imparted, all the while believing they were sipping Pinot Blanc.

Then one day before our time, suspicions arose, and Ken Wright sent the suspect grapes to an ampelographer, a person in a lab who categorizes and identifies grapes, for genetic investigation; DNA testing is not just for criminals, you know. The grapes were, in fact, Melon.

Besides being premier grape farmers, John and Martha have proven to be first-class trail guides. Together, we found flora rarities like wispy wild orchids and the ghostly-white Indian pipe; watched eagles and ospreys soar and dive; and spotted a drab-feathered ouzel scaling a pounding waterfall as if he were moving up a pine branch. Once on a hillside above the Columbia River we came on the very stone trenches where Indian youths in past centuries lay in wait of spirit visions.

That day at Silver Falls, we encountered something along the secluded trails that was even more curious—an old friend. Our foursome had just emerged from a trailhead when a familiar redhead approached from the picnic grounds.

"Scott?" I asked. Even when a child grows up in your neighborhood, he or she can be difficult to recognize more than a decade after high school graduation on a fog-veiled trail in a faraway state.

"Hi," he said, as he would have had I run into him twenty years earlier, coasting along on his bike back in Des Moines. I hadn't remembered he was living in Oregon. Sentimentality washed over me.

The remarkable part of this story is that the next time Ron and I visited this same state park, Scott crossed our path for a second time. I think it was the coincidence, or perhaps cosmic design, and not the cool mist that sent a mercuric chill up my spine.

I could tell Scott was intrigued that a couple of his parents' vintage had chucked Iowa life, waved good-bye to cornfields and ground blizzards, and gone on to buy a winery in Oregon, of all locations. He was also curious and said he'd like a tour.

"Sure," I said. "Why not help at the winery open house? It's coming up on Memorial Day weekend." It didn't matter that Scott was a rookie. We all were. He could handle credit-card purchases. Ron, Michael, and Jack would siphon barrel tastings from our first-harvest wine, which would be sold as futures. I would pour the finished wine.

Wine Notes:

WINE FUTURES?

I once had to tell a bewildered university economics professor how investing in wine futures differs from speculating in pork bellies and winter wheat futures. (Let me say, I was delighted to be able to explain anything along these lines to an economics professor.)

Wine futures allow customers the opportunity to taste from the barrel and purchase wine that will be ready sometimes as long as a year in the future. The benefit to the customer who purchases early is usually a reduced case price and the opportunity to buy a product in short supply. The benefit to the winery is cash flow. Of course, the risk to the customer is the Pinot Noir won't live up to expectations.

Imagine a product that takes a minimum of eighteen months to reach its market. We purchase the grapes from the vineyard owners in October, and the finished wine doesn't hit shop shelves until two springs later. Granted, the grape payments to the farmers can sometimes be paid in installments. Barrels, corks, glass, tanks, bins, labels, and inert gas must be paid for at the time of purchase. Cash flow is problematic at most wineries, but wine futures help alleviate that problem.

I'd learned from Dale West that a woman who lived near the winery had done a good job serving bread and cheese at Ken Wright's open houses. The only problem with Raquel, a winsome brunette, was that she spoke Spanish; I hadn't spoken *una palabra* since college. If we were to communicate, Raquel and I needed a face-to-face meeting.

I would have walked across the street and knocked on Raquel's door, except her chained pit bull took exception to visitors. Even as I crossed the street, the dog menaced, slightly raising his upper lip to bare a mean set of choppers. Retreating to my rose bushes in front of the winery, I spent an afternoon alternately clipping and looking over my shoulder, hoping Raquel would step outside. Finally she appeared in her doorway.

"Raquel?" I called. The pit bull jerked on his chain.

"*Sí*," she said, ignoring the animal and walking across the street.

Hmm. How should I begin?

I pointed at the winery. Indeed, she was aware I was one of the new owners. Somehow through sign language I gathered Raquel also knew the open house was all but upon us. And yes, she seemed to get the drift that I needed her to serve crackers and cheese on the Saturday, Sunday, and Monday of Memorial Day weekend. I'd pay whatever Ken had paid her.

"*Once?*" she asked.

"*Si. Si.*" Eleven o'clock. I was delighted by our exchange; she understood the routine.

"It's all set for the bread and cheese," I told Ron. Raquel would be our most experienced helper.

Dale West had fulfilled his commitment, plunging us into the world of wine. To this point it had been sink or swim, and we'd struggled along, knowing Dale was available to rescue us when we floundered. Now, as we'd agreed at the onset of our relationship, Dale had reassociated with Ken Wright at his new winery. Mark Vlossak, our winemaker, was contracted to work the open-house weekends at St. Innocent Winery, where he also served as winemaker. Ron, Michael, Jack, and I were on our own.

Yet we felt positive. A friend from my Master Gardener class volunteered her electric cheese cutter; together we sliced a stockpile of cheese for Raquel to serve over the course of the three-day open house. The slicer, a contraption for home use, was so overworked it became overheated; we had to slow down or risk grilling the cheese. The operation took most of an afternoon, but my new friend and I stuck, sometimes literally, with it.

I threw black tablecloths over rented round tables and placed a lavender plant in the center of each. I'd also rented a Chemcan (Portapotty, Honey Bucket, Kybo, Willy Make It—I'm not sure which name you'll recognize) and had it positioned at the side of the winery property. Our indoor toilet, although we'd been told the problem was actually with the primeval pipes, was still untrustworthy.

We hauled our rectangular oak table, the same table where the crew had eaten during crush, to the front of the winery and set a half dozen bottles of finished wines on it with a couple dozen glasses. This is where I would stand with a friend of Michael's who'd been begged or bribed—I can't remember now how it went—to help us. Michael had promised me that his friend was licensed to serve and knew something about wine. The guys strung some clear plastic hoses through the racks so customers could taste wine as it was siphoned from the barrels. At last, we were ready.

"Okay," I said as we doused the lights the evening before the open house. "Everyone be here by eleven tomorrow. I hope the day won't go too slowly." I envisioned us whiling away the hours, waiting for people to wander in off the street; we still didn't know many customers to expect. At least, we'd have each other for entertainment. Having survived crush, we were already a cohesive crew looking out for each other's needs; even those who weren't family felt that way. We'd be sharing a big moment. Our jobs and livelihoods depended on the public taking to our wines.

The parking spaces all around the block were filled bumper to bumper when Ron unlocked the winery gate the next morning. The rest of our crew entered through the back doors on the run.

"It looks like quite a few people outside," our Des Moines friend Scott observed as a white stretch limo curled around the corner. We walked closer to the window to peek at a line that had formed on the other side of the door.

"Don't open until Raquel gets here," I said. I revisited our communication in my mind. I thought she'd said *once*, and I counted from *uno* on my fingers to make sure that meant eleven. Six pairs of eyes searched the house across the street for a sign. Suddenly Raquel's door flew open. A boy about fourteen years old clattered down the front steps, zig-zagged through traffic, cut through the line of people, and shoved on the winery door, which I cracked. I feared the throng would push in behind him if we opened the door fully.

My first words to young Alfredo, obviously Raquel's handsome son, weren't a proper greeting. "Where is she?" I blurted. We needed Raquel.

He bit his lip. "Sick," he said.

My mind raced. "How sick?"

"No, no," the other adults stepped in.

I thought about all the cheddar and the frustratingly soft, murder-to-cut Gouda slices we'd packed in the refrigerator.

Alfredo lowered his head and looked down at his polished shoes. I noticed he was wearing a freshly ironed shirt. In fact, he looked as though he might be applying for a job. Alfredo straightened his shoulders. Ron nudged me.

"Say," I said, "do you think you could put together cheese trays?" All eyes shifted toward the face in the crack of the door.

Alfredo rushed by us and took off toward the kitchen. The next I saw him, he was balancing two attractively arranged platters. And, he was grinning.

We opened the doors. Hundreds of people pressed inside. Some-where in the depths of the barrel racks, I heard one of the guys gasp at the onslaught.

"Holy smoke!" (At least I think I said *smoke* to Michael's friend, my pouring partner.) Although we stood side by side, those were the last words the two of us had time to murmur to each other all day. I have no idea what anyone else in the winery was doing except for Alfredo, whom I could see from the corner of my eye, replacing cheese trays as well as the hundreds of glasses we hadn't anticipated needing.

Occasionally my pouring partner retreated into the cellar for cases of wine that he slid under our table. The two of us felt we were handling all the visitors on our own, though later I discovered that's exactly what everyone else was thinking. The day passed in raging currents of small talk and hazardous eddies of wine questions. Unlike that first pouring back in West Des Moines, I was fending for myself. All our guests—with the exception of a young woman, a sullen blonde in a rumpled sweatsuit—seemed encouraging and forgiving of me as the winery tenderfoot.

The finished wine I was pouring hadn't been in the bottle long, so it was a little tight, meaning the flavors had yet to fully emerge. We'd been late bottling and our repertoire was limited at that first open house, or we would have offered a substitute.

The blonde grump appeared just before noon, as I recall, took a sip of wine, and swallowed hard. "What does it taste like?" she demanded of me. The guests came to an abrupt halt behind her. My pouring partner paused, then went back to pulling a stubborn cork.

"It's still a little closed because the wine's so recently bottled," I said. "We think it has good potential." (Ron had told me to say that.)

"I want to know what I'm tasting." She yanked out a small spiral notebook. My nightmare had materialized.

"Pinot Noir," I answered. "This is actually a blend, but it's all Pinot Noir." I glanced at my partner, but he was distracted, pouring tastes of wine while conversing on the subject of aging potential.

The grump's flat gray eyes riveted on me as if she were Perry Mason and I were the liar on the witness stand.

"I mean, what does it taste *like*," she repeated, swallowing another mouthful.

I, of course, was observing her as she drank the wine, so I was not understanding her question. Was it possible she was born without taste buds? Was she picking up off-flavors or a strange chemical? Did her glass contain residual soap from the dishwasher? I felt like a dullard for not being able to tell the woman what she wanted to hear.

Finally she blurted, "If you don't know what the wine tastes like, *you* shouldn't be working here."

All other conversation dangled in the air. My partner set down the glass he was holding and opened his mouth. Then he shut it. I felt the heat rise from under my collar.

"Next," I said, looking at the person behind her in line. It was a blip on my life-screen, but an important one. The exchange distracted me the rest of the afternoon. She may have been rude, but I felt stupid.

People from all walks of life, including at least one cross-dresser who was spiffier in her camel blazer and pleated wool skirt than the rest of us put together, were patient with me. New neighbors and fellow vintners came by to encourage us.

One of our other troubling guests came decked out in what looked to be a hand-sewn floral dress, white flats, and textured nylons. She was straight from the pew on Sunday morning. I noticed that this young lady was twisting papers in her hands. The more I watched, the more I was sure she was ready to break into tears.

"What's going on?" I asked, breaking away from the other visitors. I touched her arm, but she moved away.

The woman was about twenty, and I thought perhaps she'd run into some kind of trouble and wanted to make a phone call. Instead, she pushed a sweaty pamphlet toward me. The subject of the pamphlet was along the lines of the depravity of drinkers. Her church, she explained, didn't believe in consuming alcoholic beverages.

I promised the visitor I'd read her information. Looking relieved, she scurried toward the door. I'm sure she felt lucky to have escaped our iniquitous digs. That night I did as promised and looked at her information. It was absolutely correct about one thing: Life hands some of us good reasons to avoid alcohol. Even wine.

Early in my life that lesson was drilled into me by my parents. They had models to draw from—including a great-grandparent who, after an afternoon of revelry with the gin bottle, staggered outside to tell his problems to the neighbor's bull.

Initially I was led to believe the only living drinker in the family was our Uncle Paul. Paul sipped scotch over slick ice cubes while the rest of us slugged back Cokes. Later, I discovered my uncle was not the only imbiber in our tribe. He was just the only one gutsy enough to come out of the liquor closet. Maybe he got away with his scotch because Paul, not a blood relative, was Methodist and the rest of us were Baptists.

My best friend in the seventh grade was a Methodist. Our church kept the Sabbath holy by shunning alcohol and, of all things, stores (even grocery stores) on the first day of the week. My mom couldn't be tempted to buy a loaf of bread on Sunday, though I was never sure how that evil could rank with the murder and mayhem outlawed in the remaining nine Commandments. Baptists like us didn't sever moral misdemeanors from the list of moral felonies.

My Methodist pal and her family, on the other hand, were free to go out for cheeseburgers after church; then they occasionally advanced to a matinee at a downtown theater. My friend called it the *the-A-ter*. So, I did too. Since I could not convince my (boring) family what they were missing, I dreamed of being adopted by Methodists.

Yet as I grew older, I picked up on a trickle of encouraging signs. For example, one Sunday while we were repeating the creed inscribed on the back cover of our church hymnals, my mother suddenly clammed up. When I asked her why—poking and whispering—she scratched out a message on a scrap of paper from her purse: "Later."

The sermon dragged on longer than ever. Though we were a small congregation, the offering plates passed from the front to the back rows at what seemed to be an impossibly sluggish speed. As always I sang the final hymn loudly and slightly faster than the music director led, hoping to propel the tempo and force the organist into overdrive. That morning I set the pace to "Onward Christian Soldiers."

In the car on the way home my mom confided—in that same tone she used on the occasions I'd learned we'd be welcoming another sister or brother—that occasionally on New Year's Eve she'd sipped Champagne; she didn't feel she could repeat the pledge of abstinence. Our eyes collided in the rear view mirror.

It dawned on me for the first time—Bible in lap, in the backseat of her blue Bel Air station wagon—that my parents lived out crucial parts of their lives in ways that didn't involve me. Because she told the truth, my mom's lesson smacked more of honesty than temperance. Even so, Paul remained our only overt imbiber.

Anyone who serves alcohol at an Oregon winery must complete a course mandated by the state's Liquor Control Commission. At the end of the day, each server must also pass a written test. Some of the questions are tricky. For instance: You are a food and beverage server at a golf club pro shop with a bar. A man and his six-year-old son enter the shop; the child orders a hamburger, fries, and a glass of milk from the menu. Dad orders two double martinis at the bar. Is it legal to serve the child?

I answered a question similar to this on the test, but have forgotten the answer because, for me, pro-shop protocol is immaterial. The crux of the course boils down to this in the winery biz: Is the server licensed, abstaining, and of age; and, is the drinker legal and sober? The question isn't who's driving home, because every adult must at all times be capable of taking the wheel. Unfortunately, winery visitors are unaware of this technicality, especially those who've forked out the big bucks to arrive by limo. This is a fuzzy area for guests even before they begin to imbibe; imagine the befuddlement after an afternoon of wine tasting.

No one who has ever worked at our winery has hesitated to point out those suspected to be looped, sloshed, or snockered, although we've only verified a few. From the beginning, we've had a system: one of our staff catches my eye, surreptitiously points to the over-imbiber, and signals the cutoff with a flat palm to his or her own throat. Sometimes I wondered if my business cards read "owner" and "bouncer." On the other hand, the indulgers were always female; so perhaps the men thought I'd do a better job with the gals. (My personal opinion is that men are seasoned parlor artists when it comes to concealing their dispositions.) According to OLCC rules, I'm supposed to attempt to remove the drink from the over-indulger's hand. These ladies may be clumsy, but they're quick. One threw her drink down her throat as I made my lunge.

"You're going to hate yourself tomorrow morning for that," I said.

"No, I'm not," she said steadily.

Next I tried the cooperative technique. It goes something like this. In fact, the following is an actual transcript of something that actually occurred. No, I'm kidding—but it's close to what happened when I approached a bouffanted babe who'd poured herself into a fringed suede shirt.

Me: *You won't believe this.*

The Soused One: *Whaa?*

Me: *Someone reported you've had too much to drink.*

I shrug incredulously.

She glances around the room.

Me: *How do you feel?*

The Soused One: *Just a little tipsy, but it's okay. I'm with . . . the limo.*

Me: *So, they could be right that you've had a little too much?*

I look shocked, as if her intoxication is the last thing I would have guessed.

The Soused One: *Couu be.*

I swipe at warp speed.

Me: *Then I have to take your glass.*

The Soused One: *Where's my friends?*

Our instructors told us that these guests will appreciate being side-tracked from their destructive drinking behaviors. Expect a call the next morning, a thank-you note, or even a bouquet of flowers, they've said. *Right.* Believe me, these people are not writing thank-you notes; they're sleeping it off.

At the bottom of the last hour of the last day of that first open house weekend, Alfredo snapped down the shades. It was over. The crowd had surged in the late afternoon with conversation rising to a roar in the barrel racks, and then as closing time approached, our guests trickled homeward. After three days of standing in the same spot on the cement floor, my ankles were fixed in a semi-cocked position. I hobbled from the table. My pouring partner's eyes looked glazed over.

"I have to get home," the poor guy croaked. We'd repeated the same phrases again and again. Though I'd had nothing alcoholic or caffeinated to drink, I felt a queasy combination of exhausted agitation. And truth be told, the blonde grump had depressed me. Perhaps she was right, and Ron should find more experienced help to replace me at the next open house.

The guys drained the plastic tubes that hung from the barrels, dumped the spit buckets, and rearranged the furniture. Ron counted the money in the cash box. Scott ran the credit-card receipts. Alfredo washed the cheese platters, as I searched for stray glasses that had been left in every crack and crevice in the old building. Suddenly fatigue overtook agitation and exhaustion and coursed through me. A person cannot live on Gouda alone.

"Let's get out of here," I said. We'd made dinner reservations for everyone at a nearby restaurant.

People checked their watches; it was just five-thirty. "The restaurant won't be ready for us for another half-hour," Ron replied, distracted with the dollar count, "but they're putting out wine and cheese for all the winery people who get there early."

"Wine and cheese?" I said. "Wine and cheese? Isn't that what we've been doing all day?" I couldn't imagine more small talk, more cheese cubes. I'd been pouring wine nonstop for six hours. (I caught a look from Jack that said, Now's another good time for those Zen-like thoughts, sister.)

"Does the restaurant have a liquor license?" I asked.

"What?" Ron looked up at me. "Just wine."

Scott interrupted. "Let's find a martini, Linda."

A martini? The thought of our neighbor boy taking me out for a drink seemed, well, strange, yet under the circumstances, utterly appealing. Much better than Zen.

Scott and I left on foot—I was limping slightly on my stiff ankles— in search of a comfortable place to chill out. Everyone else seemed content with wine and cheese hors d'oeuvres at the restaurant.

"Then we'll see you in a half-hour?" Ron asked a little plaintively. He was off to make the bank deposit, though he, too, probably could have used a martini.

The first bar Scott and I approached advertised Cherokee Jerry on the piano; even the possibility of clamorous music threatened to shatter my weary psyche. Without a word, we changed course toward the Blue Moon, a tranquil-sounding place on McMinnville's main drag just blocks from Panther Creek. Its marquee promised a New York Strip dinner for two for $15.99.

The Moon's bartender glanced up as we entered and then continued polishing a glass with his cloth. The silent jukebox radiated rainbow colors through the smoky atmosphere like a lighthouse through fog. Some regulars—a muscular Latino, a skinny cowboy in a cocked black hat, a middle-aged woman fighting a smoker's cough—stared into their drinks. Unlike the winery, this place was blessedly free of chatter. Above the bar on the TV, baseball players silently slid into first, unobtrusively made it home. In fact, the whole bar sounded as if someone had hit the mute button, and that was fine with me. At that moment Scott and I sought quiet—and a vodka martini with three green olives on a miniature sword. Scott placed our order.

We slid into a semicircular, red-leatherette booth facing the backs of the regulars perched on bar stools. The plastic-sheathed bar menu offered appealing choices for those of us who were half starved. As far as I could tell, however, no one had come to the Moon for the Reubens or French dips. Apparently we'd all converged for the same reason— drinks and contemplation.

The day's conversations ran through my brain like mini freight trains. Round and round they went, screeching to a halt at a joke or intriguing story. I thought back to the blonde grump, which caused a small pileup on the brain track.

Why had she been so rude? Everyone else had been so encouraging. What had she actually said?

"A woman told me if I didn't know what I was talking about, I shouldn't be working at the winery," I blurted.

Scott's eyes opened wide. "Maybe she'd had too much to drink."

"I should have taken her glass." I reveled in that thought.

"Yeah, you should have told her you owned the place."

"Right." That would have felt pretty good—for a minute. I also knew the woman had a point.

It was there in the Blue Moon with Scott, who for his youth was astute enough to know when an older person needs to work things out in her own mind, that I realized I'd better change course. I never wanted to feel that disparaged again. If I was going to be Ron's partner in this endeavor, I couldn't undermine him. With the oily martini floating in front of me, I promised myself I'd get with it: become as much an expert as I possibly could on our wines. I'd never have the perseverance to learn about all the world's grapes, wines, vintages, and vineyards—but I could certainly decode Pinot Noir.

Suddenly I felt invigorated, realizing that it had been the woman's criticism, and not the work, which had been so wearing that afternoon. Scott and I basked in silence for a few minutes longer.

"I wonder what they're doing at the restaurant," he said. We quickly chewed the vodka-y olives off our toothpicks, paid the tab, and scurried down the street.

The two of us arrived at the Third Street Grill just as people were taking their places around the tables. Alfredo and Ron squeezed over and made a place for me between them. Ron was exuberant. We toasted each other and the customers; I thought of the grump, whom I'll never forget.

Later that evening Ken Wright asked me how the day had gone. In the course of the conversation, I confessed my mishap and told Ken I needed to learn more about tasting. He suggested I get familiar with the aroma wheel that had been developed at the University of California, Davis.

Believe me, I studied the wheel before the following open house. When the next person asked what she was tasting, I understood that she was actually asking what *I* was tasting, and I had a ready answer. For novices, the aroma wheel is a way to discover the scads of aromas/flavors wine can impart, everything from mousy (not my favorite) to violets. Familiarity with the chart allows tasters to supplement with their own aroma and flavor sensations.

The aroma wheel was just the beginning. I began to read about the production of Pinot Noir. I asked questions at the winery, in the vineyards, and about the bottles opened in our own dining room. The truth is, I had learned from "osmosis" just by working at the winery. My body had already absorbed the purple stain.

Predators such as owls and hawks clear vineyards of rodents and migrating birds that cause significant crop losses.

CHAPTER 14

Flying High

S UMMER WAS PASSING and I was becoming more and more
peeved at the thought of our Shea Vineyard Pinot Noir being rejected from the upcoming wine festival. I had made plans to be out
of town that weekend. New to the industry, we weren't in a financial
situation to take hits. We'd dug deep to pay for the business, the new
equipment, and the repairs on the building.

"You won't even go to the salmon roast?" Ron asked. He'd bought
tickets and tried to entice me—wheedled, even—telling me how the
romantic Chinese lanterns dangled above the tables in the oak grove.

If this defined the romance in winemaking, I told him, I'd pass.

Several local volunteers asked if I'd like to donate time to setting
up the gift shop for the celebration. I found their request a convenient
occasion to spread the word that I wouldn't be around.

"You're not showing Panther Creek wine?" they asked.

"No," I said, unwilling to explain the selection process or make excuses. If Ron, Michael, Jack, and Mark all said the rejected wine was
great, the wine was great. I knew it. At least, I was pretty sure it was
great.

In addition, Doris reported that Steiger Haus had sold; they'd be
moving as soon as they could get packed. Lynn and Doris had yearned
for a new place in the shadows of the Wallowa Mountains. They loved

the stories of the land renowned for the Nez Perce hero, Chief Joseph, who dropped his weapons uttering the poignant words, "I will fight no more forever."

Soon Doris and Lynn would be testing their new terroir. Sad as it was to see them go, I wished them well in their adventure.

In some ways I'd become amenable to our life change. With both daughters gone, our West Des Moines house would have resonated with too many conversations that started with, "Remember when . . ." The move had forced me to sell the Barbie doll clothes and give away the Smurfs. The Wonder Woman bike had to go. As with the Steigers, it had been the right time for Ron and me to move on.

Years earlier a Des Moines realtor had showed me a home that was owned by a woman in her late seventies, a widow. The price was good; the realtor said the owner's son felt the need for his mom to move into a retirement center.

The living area of the sale home was well-kept, swept and dusted, though the last remodeling had apparently happened soon after the Beatles appeared on Ed Sullivan's show. I'd forgotten, fortunately, the emphasis of the color orange in the scheme of the Mediterranean furniture craze, though I have to admit the dark, heavily turned wooden pieces did work well with macramé and shag carpeting. (I can see it on the History Channel now. A scientist with white gloves holds up a torn, net-like ornament. "Archaeologists have recovered shards of beads embedded in knotted twine, so typical of the Craft Movement during the Hootenanny Era.") In the kitchen, I recognized the colored Pyrex mixing bowls and enameled fondue pot from my own wedding-gift stash.

It was the boy's bedroom, however, that hit me in the pit of my stomach. The place echoed this mother's pitiful homage to her, by that time, middle-aged child. Faded cowboy wallpaper (a bumbler in

Western boots roping a high-kicking calf) still hung on the walls. The bookshelves sagged with the weight of hundreds of dusty comic books and an old plastic radio. A metal flashlight rusted on the nightstand. The house was a heartbreaker. I saw firsthand that refusing to move on in life has pathetic consequences.

Learning about Oregon and the winery had overwhelmed most of my brain capacity, leaving me little energy to pine. Events passed me like trains on a track. Life was speeding by. We'd met Doris and Lynn; we'd become friends with Doris and Lynn; and now we were losing Doris and Lynn. But what looked like an ending was really another beginning.

The Steigers organized a barbecue before leaving, where they invited the newcomers to McMinnville—all of us who'd taken temporary refuge at their B&B while we searched for our new digs and, then again, while we waited for our moving vans to arrive.

"Now it's up to you to make friends with each other," Doris had said. Before we knew it, she and Lynn were on their way.

Fortunately in the few months we'd lived in McMinnville, we were making some inroads toward other friendships. Helen and Dan Dusschee invited us for dinner one balmy summer evening. We were actually looking forward to spending our second crush in our own house, rather than at the Steigers' B&B. Despite my dissatisfaction with the baloney house, I admitted to Helen that it would seem pure luxury to run a load of sticky clothes through my own washing machine after a day on the grape-sorting line. On those late nights, I was looking forward to collapsing in our own bed.

Ron and I were also learning the importance of actually living in the Willamette Valley where we had time during the summer to get out and check how the grapes in the various vineyards were progressing throughout the growing season.

Wine Notes:

VINEYARD DECISIONS

While the vines would produce four tons per acre, we prefer about two. Thinning the number of grape clusters on the vines concentrates fruit flavors in the finished product. Winemakers thin when they're making premium Pinot Noir; this task should be completed about the time of veraison (in late summer when the grapes turn from green to purple). Dropping fruit after that time doesn't affect fruit flavors significantly.

The farmer can also estimate the number of tons he will deliver to the winery around the time of veraison. We thin according to the farmer's estimate; for example, if he estimates three tons per acre of hanging fruit, we would want to drop about one ton per acre, in itself an estimate. Lost fruit also means less wine to sell, so it's a significant decision. The number of tons per acre is, however, always a wily figure, and we can all be surprised at delivery, which is when we learn precisely how many tons we'll ferment.

The discarded grapes lying in the rows between the trellised vines are a melancholy sight, especially difficult for the farmer who's planted and trellised the vines, pulled leaves, watched for disease, and then babied the fruit since it was just a flower.

Vintners dealing with premium wines allay some of the farmer's disquietude by paying for the acreage, rather than by the weight of the harvested fruit. The vintner takes financial responsibility for the fruit that is dropped. With fine winemaking all decisions hinge on balancing business and art, a little magic, and a lot of luck.

Now as we headed into our second harvest, we had time to learn more about how the grapes evolve in the vineyard. The Dusschees, Ron, and I traipsed around the meticulous Freedom Hill Vineyard and considered the condition of the fruit. Dan offered his best prediction of when we should plan to pick the grapes. We admired the uniformity of the healthy-looking clusters. On the way to the house we drove past one small parcel of newly planted grapes; Helen bit her lip and shook her head.

"What's wrong with these little guys?" I asked, pointing at the wilting baby vines. I would have guessed phylloxera, but I knew their new vines were phylloxera-resistant.

"Mice," she growled. Pocket gophers, deer, and migrating birds play havoc in vineyards too. More than one vineyard owner has sprained his or her ankle tripping in a gopher hole. Deer are best deterred with high fences. Migrating birds *may* be persuaded to do a flyby if a vineyard owner plays recordings of bird distress sounds; the recordings are ghastly, as if fellow feathered travelers are encountering terrible calamities. Some vineyard owners set off "cannons," which sound like gunfire. From what I've seen, after a day or so the noise bothers humans more than birds.

With the mouse situation at the Dusschees' vineyard nibbling at the back of my mind, I asked Ron if he'd enroll in a short falconry course with me. Falcons are residents of some California vineyards, but I don't think any Oregon grape farmers employ them. Yet.

This seemed to be one of my wild hares Ron could abide. We had the choice of a falcon, a hawk, or an owl, but we were encouraged to use the hawk for the lesson. The falcon was not at flying weight; in other words, had a full stomach and wouldn't be in a hunting mindset. The instructor told us the owl, a night predator, was difficult to rouse during the day. In fact, none of the three birds with their droopy eyelids looked too eager to join our novice group. I would have thought they would be yanking at their tethers for the opportunity to fly free and swoop down on a warm meal. Not so.

"It's all about food," the trainer said, pointing at our fly guys. The sport of falconry dates to the Middle Ages; then a hunter kept his birds *in trim* before the hunt. Even today, falconers weigh their birds to pre-determine how well, or if, they'll perform.

As I pulled on the bulky leather glove, the hawk we'd chosen came suddenly alert and tensed more like a cat than a bird. I raised a piece of raw chicken and the raptor, which seconds before had been feigning nonchalance in a treetop fifty feet away, plunged headlong toward my glove. The wind from its wings swished my hair. While some of our group found the bird's swoop intimidating, I found the hit a rush. I have to say I was repulsed by the warm hunks of raw chicken, but the instructor told us raptors shun cooked meat. They relish feathers and claws with their dinner. They're especially partial to dead rats. (As I've mentioned, I don't take to rats—dead or alive.)

We felt close to nature, treading the woodland paths with our hawk flying above the treetops, literally watching our backs.

Of course hunting birds demand special gear. They're easily agitated, but leather hoods subdue the predators immediately. They sport tethers, called *jesses*, and sometimes leather chaps. Chaps are important because in a fight to the death some rodents, squirrels in particular, will assault a predator's vulnerable legs. The instructor said the largest animal he's seen downed by a falcon was a doe. Imagine.

Although I had an interest in completing the highly regulated training, I knew our in-town neighbors wouldn't allow me to harbor a raptor in the backyard. Ron and I both thought the training was a thrill. I've read that when some women get old, they plan to wear purple. When I get old I may become a crone, sport an oversized leather glove, and stir up love potions in my own backyard cauldron.

Speaking of crones, I'd become witchier and witchier thinking about the wine festival. I wish I could report the festival panel reviewed the tasting and discovered they'd made a stupendous error in rejecting our Shea Vineyard Pinot Noir. If this were fiction, I'd write the story exactly that way. Unfortunately I'm bound to truth—as I remember it—

in this missive, and the groveling phone call never came. My insecurities about fitting into the Oregon wine scene escalated with even an off-hand reference to the summer festival.

Ignoring my mutinous grumbling about blind tasters (how blind is *blind*?), wine critics, and reviewers, Ron mustered his courage and sent the same wine that had been rejected by the festival panel to Robert Parker's exacting *Wine Advocate*. From what I'd seen, the reviews in this publication were interpreted as gospel by distributors, consumers, wineshop owners, and restaurateurs. I have to say I was stunned at my husband's show of bravado and what I considered an appalling case of bad judgment. All we needed was another highly prominent, negative review.

"Why subject ourselves to the critics? We're selling our wine without their ratings and rankings," I'd pleaded.

Instead of answering my question, he asked if I'd reconsider going to the festival with him.

"Right. And the first thing everyone is going to ask is why Panther Creek isn't participating." Ron and I had returned to this subject time and again. "You'll have to tell them our wine was rejected; then they'll get a pretty good idea of what we've accomplished."

Stalemate. Frankly, this subject went further than a negative review. For me, the rejection cut to the heart of our decision to buy the winery. I couldn't help but think if we'd spent more time researching the business of winemaking, we would have known that success isn't totally dependent on the quality of the product. As with any other industry, marketing, luck, connections, politics, and—in this case—personal preference can influence any winery's status in the marketplace. Our retirement income was tied up in this endeavor. But Ron wasn't willing to admit defeat so easily.

We worked and waited months for the *Wine Advocate* review. The guys held to their opinion that the wine was superior, and the more I'd tasted, the more I thought the Shea actually was terrific. Being a greenhorn, however, I just wasn't sure strangers would agree with me.

When we received the news, it came as a phone call from a fellow vintner who'd seen an early copy of the most recent *Advocate*. Panther Creek's Shea Pinot Noir, the same wine rejected by the wine festival, had finally been reviewed.

"Is our score decent?" I asked Ron. Inside I was cringing. Then I saw Michael smother a smile. Panther Creek had earned the highest score an Oregon Pinot Noir had ever received from Robert Parker's highly respected publication. My ears heard the number—but the magnitude, a ten on the Richter scale of welcome news, took a moment to joggle into my brain.

Later that evening in the shadows at the back of the winery, Ron and I uncorked a bottle of the Shea just to see. I climbed on a barrel, then swirled the enigmatic liquid in my glass.

"I can taste raspberries," I said.

Ron looked at me. "Honestly?"

"Strawberries, too."

Once I thought my tastes were closed. Now strawberries, raspberries, cherries, and currants shimmied on my tongue. I have to say no wine has tasted sweeter than the Shea Ron and I shared on that auspicious occasion, just the two of us perched back-to-back on a barrel savoring the heady blend of hard work, Ron's perseverance, and, finally, good fortune.

"I guess I should have had more confidence in you," I admitted to his back. I find apologies like chewing seeds, but there is a time and a place—and this was one of them.

Feeling Ron's sigh of relief, I could once again appreciate the depth of his attachment to the winery. Though making wine wasn't my passion, I'd come to appreciate his. While he relished the process, I realized I was becoming smitten with the history, steeped in the traditions of monks and ancient vineyards, blooms and harvests, dusty bottles and crystal goblets, musty caves and oak forests, consuming physical labor, and the gathering of friends. I wanted to thank our tipsy winery angels;

they'd taken their share (still five percent by our calculations), and now it seemed the angels were taking care of us.

We held our heads high at the wine festival; Ron attended the tastings and seminars. I joined him for the salmon bake. The Shea Pinot Noir revved sales and proved to be conversation fodder, though few, if anyone, asked why we weren't showing our wine at the festival. A number of guests visited us at the winery, luckily located within blocks of the activities.

Wine Notes:

WHAT WERE THEY THINKING?

Perhaps you are wondering how the tasting panel could have rejected a wine that another critic found so appealing. Easy. Wine, even in the bottle, is always undergoing change. The trick, whether it's for a critical tasting or a special dinner party, is to catch a particular bottle at its peak. The sample we chose could have been languishing for that vital hour during the festival tasting, even for several months, in a funk. That bottle could have had a problem of which we weren't aware: Maybe it had been exposed to heat or light. Maybe we inadvertently shook it up, and the wine was wallowing in shock (flavors in jostled wine can disappear). Or maybe, because wine tasting is purely subjective, the Shea Vineyard Pinot Noir just didn't tickle the panelists' palates as we'd hoped it would.

Meet Pinot Noir's pale cousin, Pinot Gris.

CHAPTER 15

Foraging

WINE DINNERS, which are quite different than the homestyle harvest meals at the winery or even party potlucks, figure heavily into a vintner's lifestyle. Wine dinners generally involve a series of formal courses paired with complementary wines. Foods and wines produced in the same area tend to work best together. For example, Pinot Noir complements Oregon salmon or local lamb dishes.

Ron and I practiced on thirteen sets of Iowa visitors our first summer in McMinnville. They promised that if we moved, they would follow; and these people weren't kidding. Once on *terra Oregonia,* our guests couldn't get enough of the state's bounty of fruits and vegetables. They had me swerving into wayside fruit stands, wading into u-pick fields, and waiting in line at the farmer's market for berries, cherries, kiwis, peaches, pears, mushrooms, shellfish, hazelnuts, garlic, and salmon.

Before wine and hazelnuts, the McMinnville region was known for its turkey ranches, and to this day the town stages an annual celebration in honor of the gobblers. This carnival—marked by a Ferris wheel, cotton candy, and the crowning of the Biggest Turkey (human)—charges into McMinnville every July and usurps all normal commerce on Third Street for the better part of a week.

The celebration drones on in spite of the fact that Yamhill County turkey farmers trotted off a quarter century ago. If only the carnival could have faded with the fowl. I say this as a native Iowan: in my day, the title of Pork Princess seemed something to which all attractive young women might aspire. Amazingly, however, even on the hot streets of Turkeyrama, a person can find good wine and food—and I'm not just talking turkey.

Strawberries, blueberries, and raspberries are most abundant in the summer months when the sun shines in earnest. In summer Oregonians emerge, blinking and rubbing their eyes, grabbing for sunglasses, blinded like moles by the blazing skies. They emerge, I believe, searching for berries.

While Oregon berries tend not to look as glamorous as their California cousins, they're generally more tasty and a staple of wine dinners. In other words, you should whip up your raspberry trifle with Oregon berries, then garnish with California fruit. Perhaps it's apparent I've swallowed Oregon's line that long growing seasons are necessary for full flavor development.

The marionberry was unknown in Iowa but well loved in Oregon. The fruit, by the way, was hybridized here before the racy mayor of Washington, D.C., with a similar name, caught national attention. Marionberries are giant, sweet, and practically seedless—like blackberries on steroids. Four marionberries cover a bowl of Cheerios.

The ubiquitous wild, Himalaya blackberries are also sweet, but their mean little seeds and slashing thorns make them unwanted trespassers in any yard or garden. Their canes, often the diameter of a garden hose, sneer at liquid weed killers.

Blackberries are so invasive that within a few summers they can bury a barn or summer cottage only to leave a green mound in their wake. Wildlife avoids the fat fruit because the fear of getting tangled in the briar supersedes the fear of going hungry. Recently I saw an island in a farm pond that was nothing more than a drift of blackberry canes. The water birds, ducks, geese, and a long-legged heron were steering clear of the berries, poking around for bugs on the pond's muddy banks.

Oregon newcomers tend to learn about blackberries the hard way. By late summer, a person can't walk through a neighborhood or up a country path without being seduced by the juicy fruit. "Pick me, eat me," the blackberries lure.

"Don't give out blackberry jam for Christmas presents," Karen Wright, Ken's wife, warned me that first year. "You can't get rid of the seeds." Did Karen mean you couldn't get rid of the seeds when you were making the jam, or after you'd eaten the jam?

I just didn't feel right letting all that delicious free fruit go to waste. My walking friend, Laurie, who'd recently moved to McMinnville from Idaho, and I came upon what appeared to be millions of blackberries draping a fenceline bordering a hay field. One August afternoon, Laurie and I trundled back, each carrying two buckets, heading for the thicket we'd staked out earlier that day. Ron and I were expecting Iowa guests for dinner that night. I thought I'd be home in time to make blackberry buckle. They'd be talking about me back in Iowa.

The sun was blistering, but I noticed that the berries on the outer canes, where it was sunniest, were ripest. Laurie, fearing sunburn, moved to the shaded area of fenceline at the back of the field. I ate one fat, warm berry for each I dropped in the bucket. The juice was wine-like. I began to think beyond the blackberry buckle to salads, cobblers, crumbles, bars, tarts, and tortes.

With my buckets full, my stomach stuffed, and perspiration running into my eyes, I lay down in the soft hay to wait for Laurie to finish picking. I closed my eyes.

About fifteen minutes later, I looked up to see Laurie standing over me. Sweat was standing on her flushed face. She seemed slightly breathless.

"What's the matter?" I asked. Berries tumbled from her bucket.

"Nothing's the matter," she said. "Nothing, except I thought you'd collapsed."

"Collapsed?"

"Why else would you be sprawled in this field?"

"I finished early. I didn't think about how I'd look." I pointed at my buckets and threw some berries in Laurie's to make up for her trauma.

The more I thought about it, though, she was right. I wasn't feeling well. I'd eaten too many berries. My head swam in the heat. Flies flew around my sticky lips.

"Let's go," I said.

We walked home as quickly as a person with stomach cramps can hobble.

The out-of-state dinner guests had already arrived. I managed to get the food on the table and then moved it around on my plate. I didn't make it through dessert. Even the next day, I felt a vague pain in my lower intestines where I was sure seeds were permanently embedded.

These days I'll eat a handful of blackberries, but no matter how ripe, sweet, and lavishly they grow, I can't be tempted to overdo. And, Karen was right: nobody in these parts wants homemade blackberry jam.

At Panther Creek we create food-friendly wine. I would be more help to the winery if I loved to cook. I come from a lineage of culinary mediocrity. My mother much preferred reading us fairy tales or sewing doll clothes to putting dinner on the table. And why not? When she ventured too far from macaroni and cheese, we revolted. I, for one, could sit at my place the whole evening staring down a mash of sweet potatoes, too repulsed to lift a single forkful toward my mouth. My dad couldn't stomach casseroles. It was pork chops or beef roasts for him.

Mom complained she'd eaten too many chickens during the Depression. *A chicken in every pot* had real meaning for her. Turkey was served in our house only on the third Thursday in November.

What Mom lacked in culinary achievement, she made up for in creativity with recipe names. Our favorite childhood lunch, ask any of my sibs, was called Rink-Dum-Ditty. (Boring mothers might have called this Welsh Rarebit.) Mom delighted children with her variation of the old standard by chopping Velveeta into a saucepan of tomato soup. That's Campbell's without milk. When the stringy substance is scalding enough to weld your lips together, spoon it over toast. If you're under the weather, wait to eat until the toast softens.

Food wasn't high on Mom's personal agenda either. She and her friend had to work to put on the pounds like most of us work to take them off. Their doctors had informed them that they were too skinny. I remember Mom grudgingly stirring the collar of cream back into the nonhomogenized milk. She and her friend went out for calorie-rich chocolate malts.

"Can I come? Can I come?" I begged, running after the car.

My mom pulled the Chevy to the curb and leaned out the window. "Please, get out of the street. Aunt Doris (my mom had a Doris too) and I are going to the Dairy Queen for medical reasons."

"Not fair," I'd holler at the car as it disappeared on the horizon. The doctor had recommended polio shots for me.

Recently I was searching through an old wooden recipe box that had belonged to my mother's mother. She died when I was in the fifth grade, and much as I try, I can't recall Grandma Hughes ever cooking—although she was a great one for keeping company in the kitchen. Here is a recipe I found written in her hand. My grandma was a reader, a gardener, and an embroiderer; but I realize now the woman had a shortcoming, which could explain why she seldom—if ever—lifted a spatula. This is her recipe:

Ring-Mold Patio Salad *(sounds inviting)*
Serves six.

1 package lemon Jell-O (a chic start for the '50s)
1 cup cold water
½ cup cooked lima beans (this looks dangerous)
½ tsp. grated onion (with the lemon Jell-O?)
1 cup hot water
1 cup diced tomatoes
½ cup diced celery
2 tbsp. vinegar
¼ tsp. Worcestershire sauce (what about that sunny-yellow color?)

Dissolve Jell-O in hot water and then add cold water. Chill until slightly thickened *(if you're smart, you'll stop here)*. Combine vegetables and seasonings and let stand about 30 minutes to marinate. Fold *(tell me this does not include the lima beans)* into salad. Turn into a quart ring mold. Chill until firm. ᨠ

Little wonder my mother was thin. Ron's mother likes to cook. I think that's because she could actually add tomatoes to her lettuce salads without getting any back talk. She introduced me to some tasty delights like her brisket that, I now know, is nothing more than a variation of my own mother's pot roast. Things taste more exotic at someone else's table. During harvest at the winery, I do a variation of my mother-in-law's variation on my mother's pot roast that involves beer.

The guys at the winery tell me it takes good beer to make good wine. During their few off-hours at harvest, when they get the chance to indulge, they choose to drink beer. After all, all they touch, see, taste, or smell at work is grapes and wine.

I once worked behind a Sears candy counter to help finance my college career. About two days into the job I was completely grossed out by wafting aromas of caramel turtles and banana bonbons. There I was in candy land, and none of it appealed to me.

The situation is somewhat the same during crush when the guys choose beer over wine. I bake this brisket for them, although it's also good made with some leftover red wine instead of the beer.

Beery Brisket
Serves six.

3-pound fresh, beef brisket trimmed of fat
1 envelope Lipton Onion Soup Mix
¼ cup soy sauce
¼ cup Worcestershire sauce
1 bottle of beer

Preheat oven to 300 degrees. Lay brisket in a heavy baking dish (such as a glass cake pan). Sprinkle soup mix, soy sauce, and Worcestershire sauce on the top of the meat. Pour the beer along the side of the meat. Fold tinfoil tightly over the baking dish. Put into oven and bake for 3½ to 4 hours, or until tender. Open foil carefully so as not to burn yourself on the steam. Slice the meat diagonally and discard juice. ✎

In the 1950s, Ms. Betty Crocker and Mr. Duncan Hines had nothing on Midwestern women when it came to formulating desserts. As I recall, the base of most of these confections was angel food cake. Angel food was actually nothing more than the sponge my family used to soak up the real dessert: ice cream, whipped cream, frosting, icing, pudding, chocolate sauce, lemon curd, or berry pulp. The courageous cook sprinkled jimmies in her angel food batter.

I could drive my mother wild just by touching her angel food cake pan.

"Do not, do not put Crisco on that pan," she'd say, rushing across the room to remove it from my hands. "Grease it and it's ruined." With a wrecked angel food cake pan, the family would never attend another church or, much worse, school ice cream social. We'd be outcasts.

So it was with trepidation and shock that I discovered one of my jobs would be entertaining with food at the winery. The first opportunity to entertain at Panther Creek came in the weeks just before Doris and Lynn moved away. (We'd lived in McMinnville only a few months at that time.)

Doris told me that a group of journalists had made reservations at Steiger Haus. They'd be bicycling the thirty-five miles from Portland, following the Willamette River through Yamhill County's bucolic backroads.

"Let's do a dinner for them at the winery," Doris coaxed. "This could be good publicity for Steiger Haus and Panther Creek."

"I don't think I should start with journalists," I said. *Was she nuts? I could ruin the both of us.*

I told my walking friends that I didn't feel competent having a wine dinner for the bicyclists.

"Isn't that a big part of your job?" Laurie asked. My other walking friend had come to Oregon two years earlier with her husband. They were the owners of the prestigious Cristom Winery, located a few miles south of McMinnville toward Salem.

"It won't be that bad," she promised with a pat on my back. "You have to start sometime." She'd been in my shoes—and survived.

Despite the encouragement, I was frozen. So Doris hired a caterer and rented tables and chairs. Ron, Doris, and the caterer worked out the menu, creating several courses to pair with the wine.

I felt like a slacker watching my friend spring into action, but I didn't know where to start. At this point, I'd attended only a few real wine dinners, and most were major productions. A wine dinner isn't just any dinner served with wine; it's a showcase for the chef, as well as the vintner. So how does a beginner get her arms around a six-course meal?

Doris had lived in wine country a long time; she knew just how these extravaganzas went. On the big day, I came to the winery and stuck roses from my garden in some colored glass vases I'd bought years before in France. These would be the centerpieces on the tables Doris had arranged.

The caterer was scurrying around in the kitchen. Enticing aromas drifted through the barrel racks.

"You'll see," Doris said. "This is going to be fun."

The evening was more than fun; it turned out to be exhilarating, only because we were supported by Jack, Michael, Mark, and the Steigers. About a dozen journalists chattered their way through dinner, explaining the ups and downs of their day's pedaling adventure. Mark spoke about the wines between courses, aptly demonstrating to both Ron and me how to handle another job that would soon fall on our shoulders.

I saw at least two articles that resulted from that dinner. The article in the *Wine Enthusiast* raved about the way the tables gleamed with crystal and silver (all rented). They enjoyed the food and Steiger Haus, of course. Best of all, they applauded the wine.

With practice, I learned how to sauté scallops, grill succulent salmon between lemon slices and cucumber skins (that's right, the skins), and turn ordinary raspberries into a cloud-pink confection. I developed a dinner party repertoire where I found success—and, once mastered, I stuck with it. I stuck with it, that is, until one misty, miserable evening when a dinner party went bad. Very bad.

Ron and I had decided we'd invite some wine customers, who were fortunately also friends, for dinner. I worked hard to make a meal I thought they'd enjoy—because we'd eaten in restaurants with this couple and found they were particular about where and what they ate. They inquire if the salmon is farm salmon or wild salmon, that sort of thing. I'd bought wild salmon. So far, so good.

The calamity began early in the evening at the salad course. I'd prepared a plate for each person, arranging sliced pears on arugula with a fine sprinkling of blue cheese and chopped hazelnuts over the fruit. But because I was serving appetizers in the living room first, I set the lightly wrapped salad dishes on the table on the dining room balcony, a cool, protected outdoor space where I raise parsley and chives.

While Oregon produces glorious flora, it is also home to some hideous fauna. Enter the common banana slug. The banana slug can be longer and wider than the human thumb, drips slime, and is the color of, well, a putrid banana. Apparently the slimer in question had been attracted by my parsley but hit pay dirt when he noticed the sliced pears in the salad. Because of their size, these slugs glide quickly. As fate would have it, he'd made his way on to one of the salads I was serving our guests. The good news is our guest spied the slug, or perhaps he noticed the suspicious slime trail on his plate, before putting anything in his mouth.

Our guest graciously brought his dish into the kitchen for me to check out. He closed the dining room door behind us.

"Oh, my God," I groaned. "I'm so sorry."

"It's a banana slug," he whispered.

My face burned with embarrassment. "My herbs . . ." I stuttered. I grabbed the plate and heaved the salad down the disposal. I hit the grind switch. Then I chased it with a half bottle of Clorox down the drain. I slammed the slimed plate in the dishwasher.

When the murderous deed was done, I looked up to see our guest wild eyed. "You killed him," he charged.

Sometimes I forget about Oregonians' sensibilities. I could see that our guest was in shock because I could brazenly slaughter the homely, yet innocent, invertebrate.

"I guess I panicked," I apologized. I did feel a little off-balance. Our guest knew I wasn't sorry about the "liquidation."

He said nothing at the table, though he appeared to have a blank, faraway look for the rest of the meal. I couldn't think of much in the way of conversation.

"Did something happen?" Ron finally asked. Two salads had remained untouched. I'd become nervous that the slug might have had a partner (even hermaphrodites have friends) or a slew of baby slugs.

"I'll tell you later," I said in that quiet, drawn-out manner that translates in our marriage to, *Drop this subject immediately*.

Wine Notes:

DINNER PARTY DO'S

It took me some time to become comfortable preparing multi-course wine dinners. Mostly through a series of personal foul-ups, I've developed a list of tips to which I strongly adhere. Maybe they'll help you, too:

1. **Stay simple.** There are fewer places to go wrong with a grilled steak than with boeuf à la mode—which, at least in one recipe, involves the blanching of a boned calf's foot. If you're like me and not a major talent in the kitchen, this commandment ranks Number One for a reason.

2. **Prepare with two lists.** Everyone uses a grocery shopping list. But I can't stop there. I have to make a separate planning list. What is the menu? What time will I serve the entrée? Are the napkins ironed? Do we have propane for the grill? Did I (I mean, Ron) wipe the dust off the patio chairs? Is the white wine chilled?

3. **Serve the meal in a series of small plates.** Extend the party without gorging your guests. I go with appetizers, soup, entrée, salad, cheeses, and dessert. The smaller the group, the more mini-courses can be served to keep the evening interesting.

4. **Make the table look inviting.** Try to think beyond candles and flowers. I've used seashells and my (carefully cleaned) potted herb collection. When I do choose flowers, I make them seasonal. I wouldn't decorate with mums in April or tulips in September unless we lived in the Southern Hemisphere. Sometimes in the depths of winter, even twigs can be intriguing.

   My most exotic centerpiece is the collection of carnivorous plants, mostly long-throated pitcher plants, that Michael Stevenson has given me. The mottled-purple plants are conversation pieces, and, on the patio, they keep the bees under control in a most entertaining fashion.

5. **Keep the mess to a minimum.** A mountain of greasy pots and pans destroys the mood more quickly than a scratched CD.

6. **Work ahead.** I choose recipes that allow early preparation so I can party with my guests. In most cases, they came to see us, not to see what a splash we can make in the kitchen.

7. **Get help.** If it's a big winery gathering, I need to be working the crowd, not my electric wok. And I know from experience that I can't do both at once.

8. **Be conscientious.** The tiramisu is completely unforgettable when people get sick from it. I wasn't even invited to this dinner party, but I can tell you who prepared the bad dessert. Her name is Mud.

9. **Ask about allergies.** While I was still working under eight commandments, we invited a McMinnville neighbor, a person with a nut allergy, for dinner. Much to her consternation—and then, of course, to mine—every course was laden with some sort of nut. Walnuts, hazelnuts, peanuts. I ended up raiding the refrigerator for mediocre substitutions. In addition to nuts, shellfish is another common allergen.

10. **Never panic.** I mentioned what happened with the slug.

That year in Oregon I sometimes felt emotionally lost—and part of that time, I was also quite literally lost. The confusion came because I considered McMinnville too small to resort to using a street map. Once I got within a half mile of the winery, I could look up and find the old grain elevator tower that is located across the street from Panther Creek. So in town, I kept my eyes on the sky. I was meeting people who lived on hillside vineyards and in the surrounding small towns, but I felt hesitant to venture too far from the grain elevator. I hated the jolt of looking up and not seeing my landmark.

Our daughter Allison, who was home on vacation, told me she'd already discovered some backroad shortcuts into Portland.

"Why don't you experiment? What's the worst thing that could happen?" she asked me. We were standing in the kitchen.

"I could be one of those mothers who disappears forever," I said. I was trying to decide if the dishes in the dishwasher were dirty or clean. It looked like some of both.

"If you're lost, you just ask someone. Anyone would help," she promised.

I mumbled some half-baked excuse to the inside of the dishwasher.

"Besides," she said, "getting lost is the best way to learn how to get around." Her theory made some sense. Allison had found her way around Boston that school year with no problems.

Shortly after my daughter's pep talk, I started venturing farther from the grain elevator. I drove my Miata on the backroads of Yamhill County, stopping sometimes on the deserted byways to look up at the crab apples that hung between me and the watery blue sky. Once I followed a double rainbow to the spot where the colors settled into a sweet-smelling field of mint. I ventured longer distances, dropping in at specialty nurseries—one sold orchids; another, all other varieties of tropical plants. I located a hillside B&B with a valley view, a herd of sheep, and a sunny vineyard. I came upon a marooned house that was an island unto itself at the intersection of two highways. On one back-road I found a farm where the owner specialized in herbal topiaries. He was familiar with Panther Creek and promised to rent me some of their centerpieces for the next winery open house. Once I wound up at a monastery that specialized in heavenly (sorry) chocolate truffles.

Finally, I found a produce stand with a roadside honor-jar for pay-ing. Wads of ten-dollar bills sat in the jar until the farmer trudged in from the field and stuffed the money into her apron pocket. The honor-jar impressed me as much as the vegetables, which, raw or roasted, had become important to my wine dinners. Until then, I didn't think Ore-gon could produce tasty tomatoes, but these Big Boys were as good as any I'd ever had.

One afternoon in late summer, Ron and I put the top down on the little convertible and set off to relocate this mystical fruit stand. Except for the turkey vultures hanging in the air currents above the fields, the other animals had taken refuge in the shade. Apparently the humans were waiting out the heat in air-conditioning. Temperatures hovered in the high nineties. Oregonians will stand up to floods, forest fires, and earthquakes—but temperature extremes, especially heat, send them scurrying inside.

As we sped along, Ron and I reassured each other that we were Iowans, hearty souls; heat and humidity didn't faze us. But by the time I'd relocated the produce stand and stuffed our bags with tomatoes and cucumbers, I admit to noticing the temperature had reached new highs in the Willamette Valley. Ron dozed off. I was feeling slightly disori-ented. Naturally, the grain elevator was nowhere on the horizon.

As we rounded a curve near a dairy farm, I observed a fellow strolling down his driveway, apparently to pick up the mail from his box at the roadside. Remembering Allison's advice, I pulled the little convertible toward him.

I did a double take. *Could it be?* The man seemed to be wearing only underpants. I don't mean boxers. I mean whitey, tighty underpants. He gave me a distracted wave just as I shoved the accelerator to the floor. Ron jerked in his sleep. A few Big Boys rolled out of the bag and onto the floor. The last I saw through my rearview mirror, Underpants Man was still at the end of his driveway, in the heat, in my dust, sorting through catalogs.

Bottling may be the least romantic aspect of winery work.

 CHAPTER 16

Bottle Shock

A T PANTHER CREEK, we bottle wine twice a year. We bottle our less expensive wines from the previous vintage in the weeks just preceding a new crush. Our blends are also created at this time, though not every winery is on our schedule. This timing frees up some of our barrels for new wine. Panther Creek's better wines stay in barrel for about sixteen months; consequently, in late fall and winter two vintages may be found side by side on our barrel racks. The best wine from the first crush is not on the store shelves for a full eighteen months.

Wine Notes:

MIXING IT UP

Good winemakers can improve on Mother Nature by creating blends in the weeks before bottling. When wines made from grapes grown in different vineyards are combined, the mix is considered a blend. This is true even when the grapes are all the same varietal, such as Pinot Noir. Other blends result from combining wines made from two or more varietals, such as the popular combo of Merlot and Cabernet.

At Panther Creek, we blend Pinot Noirs. The Pinot Noir grown in southern Oregon in the Umpqua Valley ripens more quickly than the Pinot Noir produced in the Northern Willamette Valley vineyards.

Highly structured wines, those with good acid and tannins, result from grapes that have benefited from a long hang time in our cooler vineyards to the north. After bottling, such wines generally require some time in the cellar, or perhaps a cool spot on a basement shelf, in order to develop their potential for more complex, interesting flavors. These wines, though some drink them young, generally evolve as they age and are worth the wait.

What would you do if you wanted to make an extra-fruity Pinot Noir balanced by good acids and tannins that could either be enjoyed young or cellared to develop into something even more intriguing later on? Perhaps you would do as we do: blend wines from the Umpqua and the Willamette valleys.

Note that I have said blend *wines*. Not grapes. The wine from each vineyard is kept isolated from the others in barrels until bottling time. All the while the wine is in barrel, it is evolving, optimistically, into something magnificent. Finally the winemaker tastes through all the wine. That means every barrel. He selects wines from specific vineyards (sometimes specific sections of vineyards) in proportions that will produce the best finished blends.

It's not inconceivable that in one vintage the Bednarik Vineyard's (Willamette Valley) peppery Pinot Noir perks up the Melrose (Umpqua Valley) fruitiness, but the next year these wines' flavor profiles change slightly and fight each other. Wines, even from the same vineyard, are subject to fluctuations in quality and flavor because of the conditions (wind, rain, sun) that might affect the grapes in the vineyard, as well as those conditions (yeast selected, temperature in the building, barrel age) in the winery. Wine characteristics induced by static conditions such as soil type tend to be less variable from vintage to vintage.

Once the wine is lab-tested to prove that the second fermentation is over and the carbon dioxide is gone from the barrel, the wine is safe to bottle. Most producers of fine wine cellar the wine in the barrel for varying lengths of time after the second fermentation.

Some wine doesn't necessarily benefit by malolactic fermentation, however. Our Pinot Gris is an example. This white wine, while loaded with fruit flavors, frequently lacks an acid "backbone" that allows it to pair well with food. Barreled, the Pinot Gris would probably come in contact with lactic bacteria, pass through malolactic fermentation, and become what we call flabby, soft, or buttery—meaning these wines lack tannins and/or acids to balance their fruit flavors. Instead, we ferment the Pinot Gris in steel tanks to avoid these characteristics. Some drinkers, especially those with less experienced palates, think soft wines are fabulous. But that's not our style.

Wine Notes:

PINOT NOIR'S PALE COUSIN, GRIS

If you order Pinot Gris (or Pinot Grigio in Italy), you'll be treated to a fruity white wine especially delicious when paired with first courses and hors d'oeuvres. Pinot Gris, like its more elegant—yet elusive—cousin, Pinot Noir, seems especially suited to grow in Oregon. The Pinot Gris grapes we use at Panther Creek are grown in southern Oregon in the viticultural region called the Umpqua Valley. Growing conditions and terroir differ greatly from the hot, high-altitude Umpqua Valley to the cooler, lower-altitude Willamette Valley. Interestingly, customers favor the product from both appellations (wine-growing areas).

We are exceedingly conscientious when we bottle wines that aren't meant to pass through secondary fermentation, like our Pinot Gris. These wines could accidentally pick up some of the lactic bacteria that's naturally on the loose in the winery. If, unbeknownst to us, a wine became inoculated with the bacteria, the secondary fermentation could begin in the bottle rather than a barrel, with the potential of blowing up on your kitchen counter. Winemakers keep wine that's not meant to pass through malolactic fermentation under sterile conditions so it won't accidentally become inoculated.

As a teenager in Iowa I had some experience with exploding bottles. I'd taken a part-time job at a drugstore during summer vacation. Though the wages were measly, I felt smug having landed inside work. A number of my classmates, seeking the big bucks, had taken field work, specifically corn-detasseling jobs. Farm jobs were tough; if the bugs didn't get you, the heat and humidity would.

In the morning, waiting to be picked up by their bus, the detasselers looked for excuses to pre-cool in the drugstore's air-conditioning. Sometimes they bought candy and chips, then waited near wooden soft-drinks cases that had been stacked under the store's massive plate-glass windows. These were the days before soda pop came in cans. The detasselers joked, they roughhoused, and they—apparently—jostled the bottles.

On one particularly hot August afternoon I was standing at the checkout counter waiting for nonexistent customers. The slant of sun coming through the windows said siesta; wafts of perfume, camphor, and tobacco whispered sleep. I struggled to keep my eyes open.

The pharmacist—I think his name was Ernie—filled prescriptions at the back of the store. To me he was nothing more than a dismembered voice like the Wizard of Oz; when we spoke, it was through the store's crackly intercom. I never would have recognized Ernie if we'd met on the street.

It happened fast, as these things always do.

Bam! Bam! Bam! I crashed out of my drowsy haze and dove behind the counter.

I ducked, rolled myself into a ball, and expected that if I opened my eyes, the next thing I'd see would be the shoes of a heat-crazed gunman.

When I dared peep over the counter, there was no other human in sight, just a brown pool of soft drinks eddying toward me. The sticky stuff was drifting under the cosmetics counter, running around a case of Kotex, and oozing under the greeting-card racks. The bottles of jostled soft drinks baking in the sun had begun to blow!

There it was again. *Bam! Bam! Bam! Bam!*

I was stepping out of the rising stream when I heard Ernie's crackle.

" 'hat's 'oing on 'p there?"

"The pop blew up," I said into the square grill of the intercom as I grabbed my purse. Fortunately, my watch read five o'clock.

" 'hat?"

I turned around, cupped my hands around my mouth, and hollered toward the back of the store, "You'd better call the janitorial service."

" 'hat?"

My replacement for the evening shift was standing inside the sliding glass door with her hands over her mouth. I threw her my smock on the way out. I had to leave. After all, I was sixteen, my shift was over, and Ron (the very one) was waiting for me in the parking lot.

As I jumped into his car, I explained the afternoon's excitement. Then for a fleeting moment I wondered if I should go back and help clean up.

"Are you kidding?" Ron asked. "You've already wrecked your shoes." Even then my guy was on the fast track to law school.

We sped off toward the local drive-in, hamburgers, and fries.

Bottle makers create extra-strong bottles for sparkling wines—and soda pop—because of the pressure the gas exerts on the glass. Notice the large punt (indentation) at the bottom of sparkling wine bottles. The punt takes some of the pressure off the outside of the bottle by disseminating the force exerted from liquid and gas inside.

We purchase our better bottles from France, and they're expensive. Cheaper bottles cost wineries about $5.50 per case; noticeable seams, unattractive colors, blemishes, and thin glass are usually the hallmarks of inferior glass. Not only are our bottles costly, about $8.50 per case, but they're expensive to ship because the heavy glass must be packed in sturdier containers. We favor a particular green-brown glass more than other colors. If you're going to produce ultra-premium wines, they'd better look appealing on the customer's table.

Traditionally, certain wines go into particularly shaped bottles. Burgundy and Pinot Noir bottles have long necks and fat middles. Chardonnay, aka white Burgundy, is put into the same-shaped bottle as Pinot Noir. When you're at the wine shop, check out the distinctive short neck and high shoulders on Cabernet, Merlot, and Bordeaux bottles. You can save a lot of label reading once you learn the industry standards for bottle shapes.

Corks have recently come under scrutiny because of their ability to spoil (or cork) an otherwise perfectly made wine in a chemical reaction that occurs in the bottle. Corked wine smells like a mildewed sponge. Further, it tastes terrible—as I *imagine* a mildewed sponge would taste. Sometimes the problem is in the nose, sometimes in the mouth, or, at worst, both. Some people can't taste corkiness unless it's pervasive. Others, like me, catch the slightest whiff and know. I'm like the canary in the mine when it comes to sensing bad bottles.

Wine Notes:

CORKING OFF

Frankly, at Panther Creek we think consumers dislike screw caps—because we do. We also know consumers dislike corked wine. Corked wine has loomed on the horizon since cork has come in contact with chlorine (as in most public water supplies). The best corks come from trees in Portugal, where the supply is dwindling. Consequently, good corks are expensive.

Corked wine (the presence of trichloranisole, or TCA) is one of a handful of wine problems even a novice can learn to pick up. Any housewife will recognize the mildewy smell, though some people are more sensitive than others. In addition, corkiness may be slight or strong in any given bad bottle. In my opinion, a very faint corkiness wouldn't be a reason to discard a bottle. The problem stems from the cork and not from the winemaker's technique.

If you're in a restaurant and the waiter presents a cork, look at it. If the cork is dried out, the wine may have been stored standing up. A shrunken cork can mean the wine is oxidized (come in contact with oxygen, another enemy of wine). Worse yet, it may be contaminated with some bacteria that slipped between the cork-bottle barrier.

Politely sniff the wine the waiter pours in your glass. If the aromas are bad (spoiled eggs or acetone-like fingernail-polish remover), or if you get the mop-bucket waft, ask your dinner partner for another opinion. If he or she thinks something's amiss, tell your waiter and ask his or her opinion. In a good restaurant, asking will probably bring you a new bottle. If not, reconsider with an open mind.

On the other hand, you don't have to drink bad wine; the restaurant can return the bad bottles to any winery for reimbursement. Corkiness and bacterial problems happen fairly infrequently at premium and ultra-premium wineries because they insist on high-quality corks.

When the flavors (tobacco or pencil lead, perhaps) of an unflawed wine just lack appeal, you're stuck. Write down the names of the wines you like, as well as those you don't. Pinot Noir, in particular, offers a wide variety of flavor profiles.

At Panther Creek, we've begun using a few synthetic corks for our less-expensive Pinot Gris. The literature we've received says the artificial corks are guaranteed in the bottle for two years. Our Pinot Gris is meant to be drunk young—but what would happen to our more expensive Pinot Noirs meant to be cellared for a decade if we were to use the synthetic corks in those wines? Would the wine's life be limited to two years? As far as we're concerned, the jury's still out. Screw caps let no air transfer into the bottle, or from the bottle into the environment. Corks are slightly porous, natural products that have been relied upon for centuries. So far, we're sticking with natural corks in our best wines.

"Is this corked?" Ron will ask, holding a glass to my nose. I have a theory that if a person has to ask, the answer is probably yes.

Like the Japanese tea service, wine service has tradition; pulling a cork is part of the anticipatory experience. The chances of getting corked wine from a chemical reaction with peroxide-sterilized, premium corks is much less than with the cheap corks.

Recently, Ron and I opened a case of some of a fabulous, though inexpensive, Italian wine recommended by our daughter Allison. Six of twelve bottles were corked and we ended up draining them into the sink. I'm sure one of the ways this winery saves money, which it passes on in the low price of the wine, is to use cheap corks.

The first year in the wine business, we purchased a six-spout hand filler to bottle and then a corker to plug our wine. With this machinery, the bottles are held under the rotating spouts by a human hand. It's a repetitive motion that must be performed in a specific rhythm or the wine sprays your shoes. Before long the person performing this task begins to notice, perhaps for the first time in his or her life, that the hand is attached to the arm, the elbow, the shoulder, the back, the thighs, the legs, and, yes, even the feet. I told Ron that because of trauma suffered in the drugstore explosions, bottling wouldn't be part of my job description. I have, however, witnessed the brave souls who work the bottling line. This job makes sorting grapes look like a child's game.

Hand labeling and foiling (placing the covering over the cork) on the filled bottles are also tricky maneuvers. Try placing sticky labels on a bottle in exactly the right spot several thousand times. The foiler on our first machinery was apparently on strike and refused to work under any circumstances—ever.

Next we tried a rotary filler, so the bottles didn't have to be hand-held under the spouts; the bottles moved under the filler on a track. Unfortunately, the labeler with that equipment also proved frustratingly ineffective. Our solution to this problem was to bottle and cork the wine at Panther Creek; then we stacked the bottles in wooden containers and trucked it to Our Lady of Guadalupe Trappist Abbey nestled east of McMinnville in the Red Hills, where the monks took over our labeling job. By offering this and other vital services (such as storage) to Willamette Valley wineries, the abbey furthers an age-old relationship between monasteries and wineries. Traditionally, however, monks themselves have made the wine and not just offered support services to the industry. One well-known example here in the United States is the old Christian Brothers winery in Napa.

The Yamhill County monks actually employed temporary workers for our labeling job, just as we would have done, but the brothers owned higher-quality, more reliable equipment for the temps to use.

Alcohol, Tobacco and Firearms (ATF) takes an interest in all aspects of winemaking, from the percentage of alcohol in the bottle to the words on the labels. For example, the alcohol level (within a specified range) must be obvious on the front of the wine label, but only in a particular size font. Not too small and not too big. Big-sized numbers might encourage those who overindulge and are nixed by ATF. Small-sized numbers might not be obvious enough for teetotalers or pregnant women to pick out. At the moment, we're removing the words *powerhouse Pinots* from our labels. We make robust Pinot Noir in McMinn-ville's historic power plant, so I thought the phrase was exceptionally clever. ATF disagrees, assuming *powerhouse* could translate to *wildly alcoholic*, which it is not.

Despite help with attaching the labels, our bottling problems didn't stop. Filling the wooden boxes and trucking the wine to the abbey created burdensome extra steps—which, not surprisingly, also involved higher insurance costs. Transporting wine involves risks.

Next we tried hiring a mobile bottler. A semi-truck containing high-speed bottling equipment in the trailer pulled into our back lot. Because of space restrictions and fear of getting drafted, I never did more than peek inside the black hole that was the bottling trailer. In the shadows I saw what looked like a small room jammed with people, a giant Erector Set, and a toy train toting wine bottles.

Ron will never give up trying to improve on this frustrating process. He won't hesitate to tell you that bottling drives him—and the other guys—out of their minds. All would agree that bottling *never* enters into the romance of winemaking.

Several new wineries have sprung up in the old grain elevator across the street from Panther Creek. Best of all, they built a permanent bottling line, which they invited us (to pay) to use. We did so by stretching a flexible pipe from our place to the bottling station. We liked the idea that the bottling equipment is stationary: it never needs to be broken down and put away. When we did this work at Panther Creek, we noticed most problems began with an imprecise setup of the machinery. A fraction of an inch malfunction caused labels to go farther and farther out of whack. By the time someone finally noticed a crooked label, twenty cases of bottles needed to be pulled. Some un-lucky soul had to stand at the sink, soak the labels off, and start over.

The new bottling line across the street worked as well as we could have expected. At about 2:30 A.M., Jack and Michael got out of bed and returned to the winery to stretch a flexible pipe across Fifth Street that ran from our place to the bottling station. (This is not a job to be tack-led while battling cross-town traffic.) As the rest of McMinnville slept, the guys let the wine trickle from our tanks into the tanks at our neigh-boring winery. Wine shouldn't be jerked around, and a gentle gravity flow is always the best means of transportation.

When wine is jostled, it can go into "shock." Then the wine's fruit flavors disappear, or shut down. You may taste tannins, you may taste acid, but this temporarily ruined wine will offer no fruit flavors. Gen-erally, after a manhandling of some sort, wine still has a few good hours before the flavors disappear. Then the wine may have to be stored in a cool, quiet place for a month or so until it returns to its original qual-ity. In most cases, a mild case of bottle shock will not ruin a wine. In fact, after regular bottling, all wine is "shocky" for a while.

Consumers can shock their wines by letting bottles bang around in a car trunk or by general rough treatment. Wine has to be babied. It's always changing; cellar wine to encourage the positive changes. The best way to store a bottle of wine is on its side in a dark environment cooled to about fifty-eight degrees. You can also ruin wine by subject-ing it to severe temperature changes, freezing it, or leaving a bottle in the sunlight. Never purchase a bottle of wine that has been languishing in a sunny shop window.

And remember, if you ever invest in a large-format bottle, like a magnum or a Jeroboam, the wine inside will take longer to age than a regular 750 ml bottle. Smaller bottles contain more oxygen per milli-liter of wine than the larger bottles. Oxygen ages wine.

Nitrogen is used during bottling to replace air in the bottles.

 CHAPTER 17

Wine Sluts, Welcome Guests, and "Affectionaros"

I INTERRUPTED MY WORK on the sorting line during that second harvest, our first as full-time residents of McMinnville, to fly back East to join our daughter Allison for parents' weekend. Ron stayed behind, apprehensive about leaving when we were being inundated with ripe grapes.

Foregoing the official parent/student festivities, Allison and I ate our way through Boston's Little Italy, shuddered at a reenactment of Salem's witch trials, sought bargains at the malls, and, best of all, caught hold of a golden autumn weekend. It wasn't until I'd kissed my younger daughter good-bye and returned to McMinnville that I sensed yet another disturbance on the home front.

Our older daughter Emily, who'd stood in for me at the winery that weekend, sounded uptight. I hadn't worn the title of mother for a quarter century not to pick up on the subtleties of my elder daughter's misplaced sighs.

"How did things go on the sorting line?" I asked her early the next week on the phone. Em was already in Seattle, back at grad school.

"Okay." *Sigh.*

"Did you have a problem?"

"*I* didn't."

"Who did?" I asked.

"There was someone sorting who . . ."

I could tell she wished she hadn't begun this conversation.

"Who what?"

"Nothing really."

"A man or a woman?"

Out it came. "This woman was after Dad."

Holy shit. Remain calm. Remain calm.

"What do you mean by 'after Dad'?"

From here, I wrenched out the story of a woman, an acquaintance of an acquaintance, who had wandered into the winery asking if we could use help sorting grapes. She said she was an experienced sorter and had, in truth, come dressed for the job. At least at our winery, a person doesn't have to present a résumé to sort out the inevitable clusters of second-crop (unripe fruit) and rot that show up even in the best of vintages.

Everyone on the conveyor gladly moved over a space. What luck; they needed another set of eyes. Dozens of bins brimming with picked, expensive Pinot Noir waited in the lot. The woman sorted all afternoon, ate dinner with the crew, and proved her pluck by staying all the way through cleanup.

"What did she look like?" I asked, trying to identify this interloper.

"I think she has dyed hair," Em said accusingly. "It was black."

"Black hair?" Who did I know with dyed black hair?

And before I could ask whether the hair was long or short, out popped the annoying part of the story: When they were finished, the woman sidled up to Ron and asked if he'd like to join her for a drink. Apparently she didn't realize Ron was Emily's father. Or my husband, for that matter. My heart still writhes in indignation as I write this.

"A drink?" Ron apparently answered. "It's two-thirty in the morning; the bars are closed." He yawned hugely, according to Emily.

"I know a place."

"Thanks, but no thanks."

Fabulous answer, fabulous husband.

"That sounds okay," I told my daughter as we continued the phone conversation.

"She came back the next morning at seven-thirty," Em countered. "With a basket of muffins."

Ha, ha, I think.

You might find your way to my husband's heart through his stomach, but he's no sucker for sweets. Scones, muffins, doughnuts, and pie crust gag Ron; he can taste the grease in pastries whether it's lard, Crisco, vegetable oil, or butter-driven. Even Pam puts him over the edge. (I've tried them all.) The muffins proffered by this cookie reportedly wafted aromas of cinnamon and ginger, and were stuffed with yellow raisins, iced with confectioners' sugar frosting. Obviously high-carb, fat-inflated.

"You know what Dad did?" Em asked.

"Passed on the muffins." I knew my guy.

"No. He said he *loved* muffins. And he took one!"

BEEP.

"Well, honey," I started. "Sometimes people feel they have to be polite even when . . . What did Dad do then?"

"He took the muffin up to his office, the crew began to sort grapes, and the woman left."

"Good," I said. I was slightly scorched, however, recalling how Ron never had a problem telling me my muffins revolted him.

So just as a wifely reminder, the next morning I whipped up a batch—the kind Ron apparently had come to enjoy, stuffed with golden raisins, drowned in confectioners' sugar frosting, rife with butter.

"Here you go," I said, plopping down the breakfast special.

Ron did a double take at his plate. "You know I hate this stuff."

"That's not what I heard," I said, as kindly as possible.

The idea of groupies is the most peculiar part of owning a winery. In truth, I never laid eyes on the muffin tease. Maybe she was a well-meaning oenophile. And maybe not. I'd heard about these "problems" at other wineries.

The more I thought about it, I realized there had already been *another* woman. The first groupie had appeared within hours of my maiden visit to the winery, before we'd even moved to McMinnville. Ron was upstairs in his office with Mark laying out a plan for the vintage: when we'd most likely be picking fruit, what equipment had to be ordered, and when Ron and I could be counted on to help. That sort of thing. I was straightening up the area at the front of the winery where tastings occurred. I'd pulled the best-looking—or perhaps I should say, the least dilapidated—chairs around the table and was bent over a dustpan when the woman vamped in through one of the open back doors. By her confident stride I suspected she had vital business, but before I could ask, she'd pulled together the very chairs I had just set around the table. She pushed three together in a row and reclined on them without so much as a greeting or a glance in my direction. With a lazy hand she ruffed her spiky hair over the top of her makeshift chaise. Then she laid her limp hand over closed eyes.

You are probably wondering what this woman looked like. I'm not, of course, a guy, but I'd say men would find her sassy, cropped hair, her tanned cheeks, her sleepy brown eyes inviting. Did I mention tight jeans?

I was completely perplexed. Her attire said this was no street person seeking safe haven. I was sweeping, but my brain was racing. What was going on here?

Dustpan in hand, I crept toward Sleeping Beauty. "May I help you?" I asked. It seemed a little late for, "Hello, how do you do. Welcome to Panther Creek." People were laid-back in McMinnville, but this woman's behavior seemed irregular on any planet. Yet for all I knew, she could have been the fire marshal, and I didn't want to burn any bridges.

She opened one eye and squinted it at me, aggravated because I'd disturbed her. "I'm just hanging out," she said. If she'd said, I'm Jack's girlfriend or Michael's sister or your new accountant, I *might* have understood.

Instead my blood pressure spiked to the roots of my dusty hair. Being the newcomer, I breathed deeply (swans swimming, clouds drifting, leaves fluttering) and waited for final verification.

"Do you know the winery has been sold?"

"I do." She stretched.

(Thunder crashing.)

"Then you'd better hang out somewhere else."

She sat up, hiked herself off the chairs, and trounced out.

Believe me, wine sluts exist, and they live, like vampires, not on blood, but on other women's wine. They float on the vapors of fermentation, drift on the perfume of French oak, and are aroused by wineries . . . or, should I say, the men—young or old, married or single, handsome or homely—who work there. Some seasons they're as common as fruit flies. Then for long periods of time, they inexplicably vanish.

The second crush passed with twice as many grapes as our first and slightly more consternation, maybe because we knew what to worry about this go-round. As soon as the winery was scrubbed after harvest, days dwindled toward the Thanksgiving weekend open house. By then Ron and I had realized we needed more crowd control. First, we reeled in our daughters to help. Then the Dusschees and their daughters volunteered. Dan Dusschee offered to give tastes from the Freedom Hill Vineyard barrels and offer a grower's insights. Helen, who knows grapes from pips to skins, replaced Michael's friend who had helped me pour the finished (bottled) wine at the first open house.

Even meticulous planning can't control bus-, limo, and van loads of visitors when they all converge on us at once. On one occasion, when several busloads of visitors arrived simultaneously, I was forced to wave down Roy, a McMinnville mailman, who, having finished his route for the day, happened into the winery to check out what was going on.

"Helen and I will pour while Roy explains how we make Pinot Noir," I told the milling bus crowd. If Roy weren't a student of Oregon wines, and if he weren't self-confident in the limelight at McMinnville's community theater (and if he hadn't asked me to dance once at the brew pub), I wouldn't have been so bold as to drag him into service. Roy entertained the bus group with vintage details—picking dates, rain delays, forecasts, and predictions—as Helen and I poured Pinot Noir. No one seemed to think it unusual to have the U.S. Postal Service delivering the local wine news.

Martha and John Stewart had volunteered to give barrel talks about their vineyard at the open house; guests have always found intrigue in their story of the mysterious, DNA-identified Melon. The Stewarts talked until they were hoarse the first and second days, but begged off the third day of the holiday weekend. They were missed more than we'd expected.

"Where's Martha Stewart?" a visitor asked as I handed her a glass of Pinot Noir. The woman's head looked as if it were on a swivel, spinning around on her neck as she surveyed the room. Definitely a type-A personality.

"She didn't come today," I said. "I think they had a family event."

"So I missed her?"

I nodded. Something about the woman's agitated search made me think she might be talking about the *other* Martha Stewart.

"You realize, it was Martha and John Stewart who were here. The Stewarts who own Stewart Vineyard over in the Red Hills."

She threw me a look that said, Get real.

"My friend met Martha Stewart here yesterday," she said. "And it wasn't some person from Yamhill County. It was *the* Martha Stewart."

Like the other Martha Stewart, my friend Martha Stewart is smart and attractive. Yet my Martha has gray hair and, as far as I know, has never appeared at the stock exchange or on the pages of her own magazine. It's not my friend's fault a celebrity usurped her name.

"I'm sorry to say you've missed her," I said. "She could only be here on Friday and Saturday."

The woman gazed into her wine and sighed deeply.

Seeing the response of visitors to the open houses, Ron and I considered eking out space for a tasting room. Much as we tried to juggle furniture and equipment, there just wasn't the square footage we needed. We did, however, welcome visitors—although we advised appointments, just to make sure someone was available to serve as a tour guide. That second fall, a memorable call was recorded on a Saturday from a potential visitor, apparently an exuberant Texan.

His broadly drawled message went something like this:

"Hello there. I was just hoping you-all would be available to give us a tour today; in fact [nervous laughter], we're right outside your door in the car. The wife and I are real Pinot Noir 'affectionaros'. . ."

Affectionaros? Didn't he mean to say *aficionados?* We didn't pick up that message until Monday morning, but Ron and I laughed on and off all week about the affectionaros we'd missed. I found the term so endearing that I began to refer to all our favorite people as affectionaros. I'd choose an affectionaro over an aficionado any day. I loved the affectionaros we'd met since we'd bought the winery—fans and fellow vintners; vineyard owners and volunteers; and, most of all, our own close-knit crew.

Do you recall that during fermentation carbon dioxide can enter the human body so stealthily that cellar workers don't realize they're overwhelmed until it's too late? In a way, that's what had happened to me. Beyond all expectation I had been overwhelmed by the people I'd met at Panther Creek. I loved the way they pitched in; I loved their stories; I loved their histories. And, believe it or not, the more I learned, the more I too was seduced by Pinot Noir—the finicky grape, the capricious grape, which crushed and fermented makes the most unpredictable of wines.

The guys at Panther Creek from the left:
Mark Vlossak, Ron Kaplan, Michael Stevenson, Jack Rovics

CHAPTER 18

A Steady Stream of Bubbles

WHEN WE BOUGHT Panther Creek, we'd inherited some barrels of base wine that were to be used for sparkling. On tasting it, we decided the wine needed another year before we could finish it. One of my favorite Panther Creek products turned out to be that sparkling brut, a blend of Pinot Noir and Chardonnay grapes. When winemakers create sparkling wine in the traditional French fashion, they refer to it as *méthode champenoise*. Brut refers to the lack of sweetness in the wine; in other words, bruts are dry. The process of making wine this way is labor intensive (read expensive): It involves an additional fermentation in the bottle and, later, a series of minute bottle rotations (riddling) to move dead yeast cells into the neck for eventual removal. We decided the next best time, financially speaking, to make sparkling wine was when hell bubbled over.

A French monk, Dom Perignon, is often credited with developing, if not inventing, Champagne; I guess historians aren't certain he literally put the sparkle in the wine. The monks at Our Lady of Guadalupe Trappist Abbey near McMinnville maintain a temperature-controlled warehouse where wineries like ours store their products before they're shipped to distributors. Accurate accounting is as important as caring for the wine. Wine is not only perishable; it's a controlled substance, so no one wants a trucker to pick up an incorrect order. The abbey is the same location where we had our wines labeled in the early years.

Some of the Yamhill County monks take a vow of silence. When I see them outside in their hooded, brown robes, contemplating in the abbey garden, I feel like a time traveler. The scene in Dom Perignon's seventeenth-century monastery couldn't have been much different.

Unfortunately for U.S. vintners, the name *sparkling wine* turns out to be a fundamental marketing obstacle. For their extravagant celebrations, customers fancy the cachet of the *Champagne* moniker.

For example, if the president called on you to christen a battleship, would you pick up a bottle of Champagne or a bottle of sparkling wine to crack over the bow? (Oops. This is a trick question, because if it's the President of the United States calling, you'd better use sparkling. Anyone else, I'd choose Champagne.)

The French prefer to keep their geographic nomenclatures sacrosanct; for us to call our product Champagne would be a legal faux pas here in Oregon. We're stuck calling what could be a completely comparable product sparkling wine. To be honest, the French would also tell you their chalky soil contributes to the flavors of their bubbly. Make up your own mind.

The sparkling wine, a seemingly great idea that wreaked havoc with our bottom line, was one of those false starts. I did, however, stash away a few cases of this sublime elixir for our daughters' weddings, as well as some for personal consumption. I don't care if the French want to call it *bubble bath*, I'm drinking it and loving it.

Wine Notes:

MAKE IT SPARKLE

Sparkling wine begins as still wine. In a good year for sparkling wine, the sugars in the hanging fruit won't be high. Pinot Noir and Chardonnay are commonly used grapes. If the skins are removed from the Pinot Noir grapes immediately after they're crushed, the bubbly won't blush. (The skin holds the color.)

In order to sparkle, the still wine must enter a second (third, if you count malolactic) fermentation in the process known as *méthode champenoise*. Fresh yeast cells are added to the still wine in the bottle and sealed in with a crown cap, like the tops on soda bottles. The wine is now considered "on the yeast," and this stage may continue for years, depending on the quality of the wine to be produced. Because the bottle is sealed, the product of fermentation—carbon dioxide—cannot escape. The gas bubbles inside the bottle.

Dead yeast cells distract from the beauty of fine bubbly, so they must be removed. We do this beginning with a process called riddling (turning). Before the bottles can be riddled, they're placed in a special rack with the necks pointed downward. For a long period of time, the bottles must be turned fractionally on a daily basis until all of the dead yeast cells fall into the neck.

Next the dead yeast cells have to be removed from the bottle. The necks of the sparkling bottles are placed in a frigid brine solution until the wine in the neck freezes. The crown cap is pulled, and a small amount of wine that holds the dead yeast cells is expelled. The winemaker refills the void in the bottle with what is called a dosage (a slightly sweetened wine solution).

A fine wine will send up a steady stream of small bubbles. The dry-ness of the sparkling, as well as the bouquet and flavors, vary as much as they do in still wines.

Just a final note about opening your bottle of sparkling wine: Remove the foil and the metal cage; put your hand over the cork (it could blow) as soon as the cage is loosened. I don't worry too much about whether I'm turning the cork or the bottle. The real trick is to lay a hand towel over the top of the bottle and start twisting either the cork or the bottle (or both) very, very slowly. Sometimes a slight rocking motion on the cork will get it moving. (If you're from Iowa, like me, you'll recognize that rocking motion as the same you use when you're trying to extricate your car's back wheels from a snowbank.)

I was seduced by sparkling wine at first taste, but I fell more slowly for McMinnville and its surroundings. The countryside outside town toward the coast is a postcard from the Old West. Ron and I spent many afternoons exploring backroads, chasing streams toward the Pacific, and gazing up into nameless vineyards. We slowed at the sight of romping lambs, kids, and crias (llama and alpaca babies).

People from our McMinnville real-estate agent to winery-business acquaintances to neighbors looked out for us; they invited us to concerts in the park and dinner parties in their homes. As a newcomer I remember the wonder of hearing my name called on a downtown block for the first time.

My new friends and I launched a lunchtime book club. Most of the original dozen members were associated directly or indirectly with the wine industry. In the book group we argued and laughed over the meaning of books, from *Corelli's Mandolin* (loved it) to *Sabbath's Theater* (hated it).

I looked forward to my daily workouts with my walking pals— even after the morning a crotchety ex-jock hobbled toward us on spent knees, raised his cane, and called us a herd of elephants. He had not lost all his marbles, just the ones that kept him civil; we *had* almost trampled him. And, the guy was right about me.

I was gaining fast. Ten, fifteen, almost twenty pounds. The only McMinnville male who thought I was cute—outside of Ron—was a parrot who wolf-whistled at me incessantly from the front porch of a neighbor's house when I passed. Wine dinners were leaving their mark—on my thighs, my hips, and, well, just about anywhere a mark could be made.

One very rainy winter morning just Laurie and I showed up for the walk. Laurie was intrepid when it came to weather. That day she was outfitted in a complete rubber pantsuit. I was a little soggier. As we passed the golf course, we noticed that for the first time, the place was deserted. Even on the dampest of days, the McMinnville golfers played through. Some donned spiked boots for their forays onto the marshy fairways.

"Let's go see the swans," I said. For once, we could walk on the golf course path without encountering golfers. When we arrived at the golf course pond, one of the magnificent birds was drifting alongside of what looked to be a beaver.

"Look how fast that animal swims," Laurie said as the beaver reeled toward us through the water. Only his head showed. Within seconds the beast was out of the water.

"It's not a, not a . . ." I whispered. My heart was beginning to pump. "It's a rat. It's a giant rat." I was backing. The animal was approaching.

"It's actually a nutria," said Laurie, backing alongside me. The animal was closing in, obviously unafraid of humans. He was the size of a beaver, colored like a beaver, in every way like a beaver, except for its foot-long rat tail. Call it what you will; the animal was a rat in my book.

"Oh God," I said. "Oh God." Within seconds I was hopping on one of the golf course benches; the rodent balanced on its back legs, getting ready to lay its paws on the bench. It was so close I could see his teeth.

That's when it became every woman for herself. I took off running, squishing through the swampy grass, struggling for speed against my weight gain. Poor Laurie also had a hard time of it in her heavy rain suit, but I was too terrorized and breathless to turn and look back. I'm not sure if nutrias are known to chase people, but this one apparently didn't think we were worth the effort. We never pushed our luck again, staying clear of the golf course pond from then on.

Nutrias were apparently imported to Yamhill County from South America, and perhaps from New Zealand, beginning in the thirties and forties. Their fur was—for a short time—considered posh, like mink. Breeders speculated nutrias would translate to big bucks. Soon, however, the fur fell into disfavor; the breeders reportedly just opened their cages, letting the giant rats—I mean, nutrias—run free. Naturally, they thrived in Oregon's moderate climate. And they reproduced. And they're rumored to run in herds in the countryside.

Okay, so I saw why it was important to remain svelte—and quick. Wine dinners, five wines, five courses, several times each week, were taking a toll. I recently found a menu descriptive of the belt-busting wine dinner that we enjoyed, prepared by Chef Philippe Boulot in the dining room at Portland's Heathman Hotel. It was the first of dozens of such feasts. Shortly before our arrival in Oregon, suave Chef Boulot had landed in Portland via Paris, via London, via San Francisco, via New York. Here's how our evening transpired, course by course:

Oregon Bay Shrimp Quesadillas
with Roasted Anaheim and Jalapeno Chilies

෨෬

Hamma Hamma Oysters
Young Leek Compote, North American Caviar Sabayon

෨෬

Sautéed Halibut Cheeks
Fricassee of Fresh Morels and Glazed Pearl Onions
Soft Mascarpone White Polenta

இ

Roast British Columbia Fallow Venison
Sweet Potato-Banana Mousseline
Raspberry Pinot Noir Demi-Glace

இ

Cheese Plate of Morbier and St. André

Now I feel nostalgic, not to mention faintly hungry, when I review this menu. Mark Vlossak poured an earlier vintage of Panther Creek's sparkling wine, my first taste. Conversation finally deteriorated to a sequence of oohs, aahs, and yums. Who could resist a morsel, or a sip?

Even on our own in McMinnville Ron and I had indulged in way too many courses at Nick's Italian Cafe (steaming minestrone followed by succulent seafood lasagna), Third Street Grill (tender rosemary-roasted chicken), Old Noah's Wine Bar (French cheeses and fruit with crusty bread), and Cafe Azul (pork with spicy Oaxacan molé sauce). We'd never found food like this in Des Moines, and our weight gain reflected our fun.

One evening when we were back at the Heathman with a group of wine distributors, Chef Boulot sent us a tray of complimentary hors d'oeuvres. Unbridled then, we chose hearty entrées from the menu; after all, we'd been traipsing around the vineyards all afternoon. To top dinner off, our waiter carried out a tray of lavish desserts for every member of our party: berry tarts, oozy chocolate cakes, bread puddings, crème brûlées, maple-pecan pie—all in all, a selection of spectacularly seductive creations. Finally one of the distributors pulled out his white handkerchief and waved it in the direction of the kitchen. We surrendered; no one could swallow another bite.

When we doddered out of the dining room, a man who was sharing an entrée with his wife yanked on my sleeve as I passed him.

"What kind of people are you?" he asked.

"Vintners," I said.

His confused look changed to one of understanding as if the empty trays, dozens of plates, glasses of Pinot Noir, and the flag of surrender now made perfect sense.

"Are you happy here?" asked my red-headed gal-pal Kathleen who was visiting from Des Moines. Back in Des Moines Kathleen lived with her family and a small pack of porcelain Staffordshire dogs who never, obviously, jumped up on her pretty chintz chairs. We'd shared many a lazy summer afternoon on her breezy porch and winter evening in front of her fireplace. Through the years Kathleen cultivated a yellow rose bush I'd coveted since the first time I saw its blowsy blooms. I'd been the beneficiary of many a bouquet.

I placed the sundial she'd brought as a housewarming gift on a rock in my McMinnville garden and we turned it and checked our watches until the dial's shadow darkened the precise hour of the day.

We both looked toward the baloney house and sighed.

"Lots of people like new construction," she said, tying her hair back in a scarf.

"It's just that I never really have," I said. "But, I'm beginning to love my garden."

We walked around to the back of the house where autumn-weary pink hollyhocks still brushed the roof tiles. She'd plucked the seeds from plants in her own backyard and given them to me, wrapped in a little red metallic packet at Christmastime, the previous year. I'd planted the seeds in the spring, as soon as Ron and I had planted ourselves in McMinnville. Somewhat aghast at the hollyhocks' size, we squinted upward as Jack must have gaped at the beanstalk.

"Do you ever think about moving back to Des Moines?" Kathleen had her eye on a house in her neighborhood for us. We could still slip back to our old digs, eat a little crow—God knows, I'd eaten everything else—and resume our previous lives.

But my answer was no. By then I was sure; the winery, our new friends, and Oregon's laid-back lifestyle had grown on me. Kathleen and

I had just returned from a picnic on the Pacific shore; the day before we'd hiked between waterfalls in the Columbia Gorge; we'd stood in a vine-yard. Finally, we'd shared a laugh-happy lunch with Ron, Michael, and Jack at Cafe Azul. Kathleen had always been fond of Ron, and now I could tell she liked Michael and Jack. She'd helped me set up a wine dinner at Panther Creek, and said she saw what I liked about Oregon.

From our yard we watched some sheep meander out of an oak grove into the green field at the end of the road.

"It's a pretty view," she said. I had to admit she was right. That same field had blossomed brilliant red in May with clover.

Chester the cat reclined in the sun on our front porch. Chester hadn't missed a beat; I'd never seen an animal make such a smooth tran-sition. Surly and unpopular in West Des Moines, he'd made chums among McMinnville's feline population. Though an oldster in cat years, he whined to go outside; once freed, he skulked around with several neighborhood cats who behaved like young toughs defending their turf.

"Have you made many friends?" Kathleen asked. I told her the wine business was a good way to meet people, but Doris and Lynn, our first acquaintances in McMinnville, had recently sold their B&B. Doris's friendship had soothed my homesickness on more than one occasion. We were making other friends, though, people I enjoyed—my walking pals; our hiking friends, the Stewarts; grape growers and other vint-ners.

"I have to admit, I'm more drawn to Portland than McMinnville," I said. "There's so much to do in Portland . . . but we wouldn't want to move the winery."

Like a Siren, the big city to the northeast whispered my name. On weekends I'd been shanghaiing Ron and releasing him in the mazelike isles of Portland's Powell's, the largest bookstore west of the Missis-sippi. I escorted him to restaurants specializing in Spanish tapas, Irish stew, Thai curry dumplings, deli pastrami sandwiches, bentos and bar-becues. I introduced him to the five thousand tranquil acres of the city's Forest Park, stepping over trillium and yellow violets, and then we wiled away the afternoons shopping the boutiques on 23rd Avenue. We took in Broadway plays, concerts, and literary events. Besides, we had wine business to take care of in Portland.

Heads spinning, we returned to McMinnville. I found reasons to visit Portland several other days each week—except during harvest, of course. Missing my old copywriting and newspaper assignments, I'd signed up for a yearlong, novel-crafting course at Portland's Marylhurst College, and then I joined a writing group there.

"You'll find a compromise," Kathleen said. Perhaps all it took was someone to plant the idea of compromise in my mind.

Within a month or so Ron and I had purchased a tiny condo, a second-floor suite that overlooked a grove of wild cherry trees on the edge of Portland. I filled it with romantic, shabby chic furniture I scrounged at flea markets, antique auctions, and garage sales. The two-room condo solved several problems. Most important to me, we could take advantage of the options the bigger city offered. When we had a late wine dinner in Portland, Ron and I no longer had to check into a hotel to escape fighting an hour of late-night traffic on dangerous Highway 99. Early-morning airline flights no longer presented a problem. Now we had a place of our own in the city to change, shower, and even spend the night—and then we could go home. Home to McMinnville, that is, where I joined the women-only gym—and began to write again.

Here's the third axiom of the universe revealed to me in this adventure: When you make momentous life changes, some fine-tuning (often in the form of compromise) is probably going to be necessary. Fortunately for both Ron and me, the winery was, at last, humming along.

"Terroir" embodies all the vineyard elements affecting the fruit.

Veraison is the time when the hanging grapes change color in the vineyard.

Epilogue: Veraison

TEN VINTAGES HAVE PASSED since we purchased Panther Creek in the weeks that waned before that incredible first crush. Had we known what we were in for, we would have rested up. At the very least, we would have visited vineyards and checked in with other vintners before we jumped into the venerable art of winemaking. That first-crush ignorance truly was bliss. Then we learned that Mother Nature is an unrelenting adversary. It pays to work with her; you'll never beat her. And in these ten years I've come to love the challenge of making fabulous Pinot Noir—and learned more about wine than I ever thought possible for a girl who hailed from a family of Iowa teetotalers.

Vintners and winemakers sort the years in their collective memories by the condition of the grapes when they arrive at the winery. Under-ripe, over-ripe (dessicated), high or low sugared, high or low acid, botrytized, sunburned, or—more infrequently—exquisite fruit remains in the brains of workers who coax grapes from vine to wine. At first I was befuddled by our new friends' flawless recollections of the picking seasons. How did they remember the hot September harvest of 1987? How did they recall the late bloom in the spring of 1991? I had such a flighty memory that I was forced to count backwards to figure what years my own daughters were born. Quickly I learned that so much tension surrounds the crush that winery workers *can't* forget the weather or condition of the grapes of a particular vintage, even when they'd like to.

As soon as the wine was in the barrels our first year, the press predicted the 1994s would be the best Oregon vintage ever. Wine reviewers seem to check weather conditions at the time of harvest and predict the vintage from there. The condition of the grapes when they arrive at the winery is only the first, although crucial, step in creating fine wine. With typical beginners' luck we nailed the 1994 vintage. Though the winery's capacity is seventy-five hundred cases, we produced what amounted to a trial run of only twenty-eight hundred that first year. If only we'd made more. We were lucky, but not so smart.

In 1995 when it started to rain, the critics panned the vintage even before the grapes fell into the destemmer-crusher. Though the press dismayed us with their negative predictions, some of our 1995 wines have aged better than the '94s that seemed so luscious at the get-go. It's a guess, but the fine, lasting quality of the 1995 vintage may be attributed to higher acids than in the 1994s.

Struggling to beat predictions of rain, we processed one hundred tons of fruit between October 9 and October 12 in 1996. I remember that harvest like those photographs that capture motion with wavy lines behind the moving objects. I can see the guys on the sorting line, peering into the destemmer-crusher, jamming the pitchfork into the stack of discarded stems, hosing down the equipment, and then all of us starting over and over and over again. I see Michael tearing around on the forklift.

Mark moved like a lightning bolt between the two wineries because, like us, St. Innocent didn't want to be caught with rain-bloated fruit. We finished sorting and crushing around 2:00 A.M.——only to begin again the next morning. The storms hit in earnest late in the day on October 12, after our last load had been delivered. When all of the fruit comes in *en masse*, the loads pass through fermentation and need to be pressed at approximately the same times too. The long hours continued well beyond the initial four days of crushing.

The 1997 vintage goes down as a turning point at Panther Creek, a literal watershed. At the winery Ron and I call 1997 difficult; around our dinner table at home we call it disaster. Mother Nature was laughing at us, not with us. A promising harvest suddenly turned sour when the fall rains started early—and for our purposes, never let up. Fearing rampant botrytis, we picked as soon as the grapes seemed physiologically ripe. Unfortunately, the flavors hadn't fully materialized, and were not what we would have preferred.

Trying to enhance the flat flavors, we put the crushed grapes through a protracted cold maceration (soak), hoping to extract whatever goodies were available. Instead of gaining beautiful flavors, we extracted so many tannins from the grape skins that a good portion of our 1997 wine was out of whack for years. Because of those strong tannins, however, the vintage cellared fairly well; for those who waited, the 1997s are just now coming around and becoming quite pleasant.

The 1997 vintage was disturbing to all of us. Mark took off for Burgundy to get fresh French insights into the situation we'd encountered. Soon after, Ron and I began to worry about selling wine for the first time since we'd bought Panther Creek.

In the early years our challenge was finding a distinctive style of winemaking and creating beautiful wines within that style. Initially, marketing was a process of allocation to a network of distributors. Ron and Mark had begun to notice that not only were many new vineyards producing grapes, but other wineries were producing a veritable sea of wine. At Panther Creek we purchase grapes from Oregon's top vineyard owners who could sell to any number of wineries. Consequently, the price of grapes and the cost of making wine hasn't decreased for us in spite of the numbers of new vineyard owners who call to tell us about the competitive prices of their grapes. Sometimes supply and demand isn't as simple as basic economics would have us believe.

Our supply of the first vintages was less than demand. A dream situation. Change, however, loomed in the wine industry—and we projected that without promotion, we'd face challenges selling all our wine within a few vintages. By the late '90s, Panther Creek wines had gradually evolved from an inherited style into a style all its own: robust Pinot Noirs with the capacity for early drinkability, as well as cellaring. Early on, we hadn't much cared whether our wines were pleasurable in the present; we'd been concentrating on creating preeminent cellared wines. Customers seemed to favor a wine that could be enjoyed immediately. Somehow, our job was to strike the right balance.

Mark contended that as far as marketing goes, every winery needs an image in the form of its winemaker. And the face at Panther Creek could *not* be his; his first commitment, as we knew from the start, was to St. Innocent. Ron and I also had discovered we needed a full-time, in-house winemaker who could guide us every hour of harvest, especially in the tough times.

"But by then the evolution had already taken place," Mark says. "It was a *fait accompli*." Who was the person who had risen to the task? Michael Stevenson.

Michael, a voracious reader and quick study, had learned what there was to know to carry Panther Creek to the next level of premium winemaking. He'd enrolled in classes, watched Mark, visited other wineries, and learned from those winemakers. In hindsight, Ron and I realized our young cellarmaster had made a lot of sense in the ideas he'd thrown out during the stressful 1997 crush.

Today Michael's import is more extensive than merely making Panther Creek wine. The public demands the winemaker at pourings and dinners. Critics and reporters want to ask questions of the winemaker. Ron and I promote Panther Creek wines, but we're usually second favorite to Michael; Michael, and Mark before him, reigns in our winery. Sometimes our friends are surprised at this information and ask Ron why he doesn't make the wine. Ron usually jokes that he's not in the habit of buying a watchdog to do the barking himself. The truth is, as I mentioned previously, the winemaker's magic is a gift very few share.

"Michael has earned his dream of making Panther Creek wines," Mark told us.

Michael's first order of business was talking us into selling our small barrel presses and making the investment to purchase a thirty-hectoliter press (which holds 3,000 liters of wine and solids). That technology alone catapulted us from a literal medieval winemaking operation into the twenty-first century. Putting 2,300 gallons of must (the capacity of a single fermentation tank) through the small barrel presses involved six loads per tank, with four to six cellar workers working full-tilt. Each load required a sticky, backbreaking process of filling, packing, pressing, and cleaning.

The new press handles all the solids from a full 2,300-gallon tank at a time. Michael can curtail or continue the pressing in mid-program according to the amounts of flavor and tannins being extricated from the skins.

Mark Vlossak remains as Panther Creek's consulting winemaker and continues to help us solve some of our most vexing problems. He's become our diagnostician.

Since 1998 we've enjoyed warm, sunny days in October with the requisite cool nights that portend a great harvest. Only an occasional passing rainstorm has heightened our anxiety in recent vintages. When the rains have come, they've blown in and out quickly; the fruit has benefited from the long hang-times that allow flavors to fully develop, the signature of Oregon Pinot Noir.

In the year 2000 we officially hired Jack as our marketing manager. Jack, believe it or not, helped us on a regular basis from year one with whatever winery work needed to be done—without pay. Sometimes I'd come into the winery and Jack would be tinkering with the refrigeration system; then he'd stand on the sorting line for a twelve-hour shift. He volunteered at every open house. He gave tours and tastings.

We desperately needed his help, but couldn't afford to put a new hire on the payroll until 2000.

I've come around to the idea that we must send our wines for tastings and ratings. Panther Creek has earned our share, including rankings in both the *Wine Enthusiast* and *Wine Spectator*'s lists of the top one hundred wines in the world. In 2000 Ron gladly served as president of the International Pinot Noir Celebration, the festival that rejected our Shea Vineyard Pinot Noir that first year.

When it comes to marketing, the number of distributors across the United States has dwindled recently because of consolidations. The trick for a small winery like ours is to find a distributor who has a niche for an ultra-premium Pinot Noir in his book. Because we're small, we must enhance the distributor's mix of wines—or we'll get lost in the shuffle. It's an international business these days. As I write, Michael is on a plane to Atlanta; Jack is planning a sales trip to China.

Together, Jack and I are seeking to get the winery building historic status. This distinction should significantly reduce our property taxes. I'm intrigued by the thought of those two massive diesel turbines that sat near the front door in the early 1900s when the winery was the city power plant. Imagine how quickly the romance dimmed when fireplaces, candles, and kerosene lamps were the *only* choices on winter nights in this northern latitude. Imagine how electrification changed lives. This building, despite a leaky roof and antiquated plumbing, has history.

We generally see Alfredo twice a year. He's employed as an advocate for migrant workers in the McMinnville schools, but he's never missed a Panther Creek open house. A few years ago we were out to dinner during Memorial Day weekend. You guessed it, we were all crammed together in the semicircular booths at the Blue Moon, deciding who was going to choose the French dip and who would share the $15.99 New York Strip dinner for two. I was studying the menu.

"I'm legal now," Alfredo said.

"Legal? What's that mean?" I asked.

"I can drink. I'm twenty-one."

When could he have grown so old? All of us raised our glasses to our friend.

Alfredo took a sip and turned up his nose. "This wine has too much going on," he reported. His review made us laugh.

"He's right," Ron said, looking at the label on the bottle he'd brought in. "This wine has too much fruit and too little acid to stand up to Alfredo's steak."

My favorite time of year is veraison when the hanging grapes are reaching maturity; the berries on a single bunch vary from chartreuse to purple. Excitement about the vintage peaks at this stage; it's our last chance to decide whether we should drop fruit. (Fewer clusters on the vine generally make for a more concentrated wine. On the other hand, dropping fruit creates a smaller harvest and less wine to sell.) Tension rises with the color change; harvest looms.

We purchased the winery in August 1994 during veraison, so I guess it's natural that this is the time when I reflect, take stock of my changed life. I remember holding my breath as I looked over the golden hay fields to the hillside vineyards that first summer, wondering what would become of Ron and me.

Veraison was upon us again in the summer of 2002 when our younger daughter Allison and her fiancé Jeremy Schubert were married in the woodland garden of a historic hotel set at the gateway to the Columbia Gorge. At dusk we held sparklers against the summer sky and sipped the sparkling wine I'd stashed away for just this occasion. In the waning twilight with family, a few of our new friends, and a sprinkling of our old friends, we toasted the newlyweds with our own wine. The sweetness of the moment did not escape me.

Before the bubbles were off that wine, in the weeks before bud break in the spring of 2003, our older daughter and her fiancé Dave Petterson were married at the winery. Though I favored the marriage, I was opposed to staging a wedding at the winery.

"For gosh sakes, who wants to come to a wedding and use a portable toilet?" I pleaded with Emily. I envisioned a hundred people after the hour-long drive from Portland standing on line, waiting for a flush.

"They aren't coming to use the bathroom," Emily countered.

When I mentioned the industrial look of the winery or the lime-crusted walls, she said that's exactly the atmosphere they sought. The winery obviously had fond memories for Dave and Emily, who like Jeremy and Allison, had spent many hours working there. They counted the Dusschees, Alfredo, and our Des Moines neighbor Scott among their close friends.

"How about the Portland rose garden?" I suggested. Now there was natural atmosphere. "Have you seen that view?"

Emily shook her head. "The problem is, we really want to be married at the winery."

"It will be nice," the florist, Lynda, promised. If Lynda hadn't done so well at Allison's wedding, I would never have put all my posies in her basket.

"Please don't fail me," I begged her. I couldn't grasp the vision, much less share it. Jack, Michael, Ben (our part-timer), Ron, the wedding planner, Emily, Dave (the groom), Dave's dad, Dave's dad's friend, and I were milling around, checking out the space and the contrived way we'd have to set the rented chairs so all the guests could see the couple take their vows.

"I could get together a little gazebo-like structure," Ben volunteered. "I mean, if you'd like it."

The florist liked it; I wasn't sure. On the wedding day I dashed, an hour late because of a wedding-gown button glitch, into a winery/spring glade. Lynda, the florist, had succeeded; the place even smelled like spring. Michael and Jack had scrubbed the building from the lab to the front door; every grape seed that had ever thought of skittering across the floor had been tracked down and reckoned with. Twinkle lights sparkled through boughs of curly willow, effectively hiding the crumbling walls; massive sprays of forsythia decked Ben's gazebo. White candles flickered on mirrored bases. The guests were not confused by the crazy seating and the only line I saw was the receiving line. To the best of my knowledge, the toilet did not overflow.

After the vows, as we greeted the final guests, a stranger peeked in the open door and said, "It's so pretty in here." A gentle rain, typical of March in Oregon, was washing over a cluster of daffodils I'd planted to brighten the dormant rose bushes. "I didn't know you did weddings."

"We don't, except for immediate family," I replied, not wanting to get the rumor started. "We're really just a working winery here." Then we were on to the reception.

While I'd been thrown by the wedding at the winery, a few weeks earlier Ron had balked at the idea of a band at the reception. "I hate dancing," he'd said when he'd heard the news that Emily had hired a band.

"Emily, Dave, and their friends apparently like it," I said.

"Then they should dance."

"But you have to dance with the bride when she's your daughter."

"Not necessarily."

"What do you mean, 'Not necessarily'?" I had a mother-of-the-bride book, stuck up with sticky notes, stuffed with papers, which was my etiquette bible. "Shall I get the book?" I threatened.

The band leader had told Emily his price included dance lessons.

"I'm not dancing, and I'm not practice-dancing," Ron said.

"Not for me, but for Emily," I countered.

It was already dark outside when we arrived at the home of the future bride and groom. They had moved all the furniture from their dining room to create a mini-ballroom for our lesson. I'd like to say Ron loosened up after a glass of his favorite Pinot Noir, but exactly the opposite effect took hold. He turned semi-rigid, unable to lift his feet.

The band leader, aka the dance instructor, launched into a series of dips, spins, and lifts—disconcerting all of us. He oscillated around Ron, who remained stationary as a floor lamp in the middle of Emily's dining room.

Yet on the big night the father of the bride swayed gracefully with his daughter, her long skirt hiding his planted feet, and later Ron had the patience to stand on the dance floor with me once or twice. Being unaccustomed to a partner who was actually in motion, I trampled all over the father of the groom.

We toasted the bride and groom with one of the last cases of the Panther Creek Sparkling Brut we'd held back for our daughters' weddings. Helen Dusschee and I danced the last dance, "Going to the Chapel," though naturally I went home with my own not-going-to-dance-again-for-the-rest-of-his-life, my honest-to-goodness first crush, Ron.

Glossary

agribusiness. The marketing and financial side of agriculture.

agronomist. An expert in agriculture.

alluvial. Soil that has been moved by water.

ampelographer. A person who identifies and categorizes grapes.

angels' share. Wine that evaporates from the barrels in a winery.

appellation. Wine-growing region, such as Willamette Valley.

aromatics. Nose or bouquet.

Bandol. Generally a bold blend of French wines incorporating the Mourvèdre grape. Also, an area in France.

barnyard. A bouquet and flavor profile many oenophiles favor.

Blanc de Noirs. The French phrase that means *white of blacks*. This white Champagne or sparkling wine is made with red grapes.

blend. Combination of wines from different vineyards, or even sections of a single vineyard. Note that blends are created by combining finished wines, not grapes.

botrytis. A mold that grows on ripe grapes in warm, damp autumns.

bottle shock. A condition in which aromatics and taste in a wine shut down temporarily because the wine has been jolted either in bottling or in handling the bottle.

bouquet. Wine aromatics, also known as nose.

brix. A measure, revealed on a refractometer or hydrometer's scale, of the percentage of sugar the fruit contains.

brut. A dry sparkling wine.

bugcatcher. A coarse filter on bottling equipment.

bung. The stopper in a barrel.

Burgundy. Pinot Noir is known as Burgundy when it's produced in that region of France. White Burgundy is made from the Chardonnay grape.

Cabernet (Franc or Sauvignon). Varieties of grape and name of this red wine when made in the United States. Wine from this grape is called Bordeaux when it's produced in that region in France.

cap. Solids (seeds, skins, and pulp) that get pushed to the top of the liquid in tanks or bins by carbon dioxide during fermentation.

carbon dioxide. A byproduct, along with heat, of fermentation.

Champagne. Sparkling wine is Champagne when it hails from France's Champagne region.

chaptalize. A process of adding sugar to juice to either sweeten the resulting wine or to boost its percentage of alcohol.

chewy. Description of a wine's texture.

clone. A hybrid of a grape varietal.

Concord. A variety of red grape, not *Vitis vinifera*.

cooper. Barrel maker.

corkiness. Description of a mildewy off-flavor and/or nose that begins in the cork and enters the wine.

Côte d'Or. An area of France located at a similar latitude as Oregon's Willamette Valley that is also known for Pinot Noir, aka Burgundy in France.

crush. The word synonymous with harvest in the wine world; the first step in making wine is often, though not necessarily, crushing the grapes.

dessicated. Overly ripe, dried-out grapes.

destemmer-crusher. A machine that removes the stems from the grape clusters and then crushes the grapes before fermentation.

dosage. A sugar syrup added along with wine that is used to fill empty space in a bottle of sparkling wine. The void is left when the dead yeast cells, and accompanying wine, are frozen and removed. The sugar syrup is used to bring the level of sweetness of the sparkling wine to that desired by the winemaker.

dry. Wine with very little residual sugar. Not sweet.

earwigs. Devil insects with pincers that come to earth directly from hell.

fermentation. The process of changing fruit sugar to alcohol.

finish. Flavors that linger after the wine is swallowed.

flabby. Description of a wine that lacks acid and tannins.

foil. The material covering the cork on a wine bottle.

foxy. A negative descriptor of a wine's nose when the aroma is reminiscent of wet fur.

frizzante. Slightly sparkling Italian wines.

gravity flow system. A gentle, favored means of moving wine in a winery that doesn't involve using a pump.

Grenache. A dark-red wine; the grapes are often grown in Spain, France, and Australia.

head. Top of a barrel.

head trained. Grapevines that are not trained on trellises.

hot. Description of a wine that tastes high in alcohol.

inert gas. A gas that doesn't react with the wine.

in trim. The state of a bird of prey when it's hungry enough to hunt.

jesses. Leather tethers used in falconry on birds of prey.

lactic acid. The result of malolactic fermentation. See **malic acid**.

lactic bacteria. Bacteria that triggers malolactic fermentation.

lees. Solids at the bottom of a bin, tank or barrel.

macerate. Soak.

malic acid. The acid in wine that changes to lactic acid during malolactic fermentation.

malolactic fermentation. The bacterial transformation by which sharp malic acid, as found in a green apple, changes to more palatable lactic acid, as found in milk.

Maréchal Foch. A variety of grape, though not *Vitis vinifera,* grown in the Midwest.

Melon. A white variety of grape known in France where it grows in the Loire Valley as Muscadet and as Melon de Bourgogne in Burgundy. The wine is also called Melon in the United States.

Missoula floods. Torrents of water that submerged the Willamette Valley when dams in a gigantic glacial lake located in the area of Montana gave way during the ice age.

mouth. Taste and texture (mouth-feel) of wine.

must. A mash of seeds, skins, pulp, and juice that comes from the destemmer-crusher and is put into tanks or barrels for fermentation.

nose. Wine aromatics, also known as bouquet.

oenophile. A person who loves wine.

on the yeast. Description of the period when yeast is enclosed in a bottle of still wine that is becoming sparkling.

phylloxera. An aphid, now found in Oregon vineyards, that nibbles on *vinifera* roots and eventually kills the plants.

Pinot Blanc. White wine or the grape of the same name, related to Pinot Noir.

Pinot Gris. A white wine made with a gray-colored grape of the same name in the United States, which is related to Pinot Noir. Also popularly known as Pinot Grigio in Italy.

Pinot Noir. A variety of red grape. The wine from this grape is also called Pinot Noir in the United States. In France, this wine is called Burgundy.

pomace. The tightly packed skins and seeds left after pressing wine.

Pommard. A Pinot Noir clone.

pressing. A step in the winemaking process before barreling when seeds, skins, and pulp are squeezed off the wine.

proprietary yeasts. Purchased yeasts, as opposed to wild yeasts.

punch down. The process of pushing the cap into the fermenting wine to improve the color and the flavor of the finished product.

punt. Indentation on the bottom of a bottle that increases its strength.

rack. To move wine with a pump, leaving the lees at the bottom of the container (tank, bin, or barrel).

refractometer. Measures sugar levels of fruit in degrees brix.

residual sugar. Sugar left unfermented in the wine.

riddle. To rotate a sparkling wine bottle so that dead yeast cells fall into the neck.

Sangiovese. The primary grape component of Italy's famous Chianti wine.

secondary fermentation. See **malolactic fermentation**.

second crop. Unripe clusters of fruit sorted out on the conveyor belt.

shelftalkers. Reviews and comments stuck on or beneath bottles at the store.

soft. Description of a fruity wine without a tannin or acid backbone.

staves. Long pieces of wood that fit together to create the sides of a barrel.

tannins. The chemicals from grape seeds, skin, or stems that allow wine to age well. Young, strong tannins create an uncomfortable, dry feeling on the palate.

terroir. All the conditions in a particular area of a vineyard—from soil type, to the direction of the prevailing winds, to the amount of annual rainfall.

thief. A tool that looks somewhat like a turkey baster used to remove wine from a barrel.

tight. Description of a wine that's lacking aromatics and/or flavors. It might be tight because the wine is shocked.

topping wine. Wine used to replace the wine that evaporates from barrels.

trellis. The post-and-wire systems used to train grapes in the vineyard.

Umpqua Valley. An Oregon wine region in the Roseburg area that runs south of the Willamette Valley, following Interstate 5 to the southernmost wine-growing region of the state, called the Rogue Valley.

veraison. The period in the ripening process when grape color turns from green to purple.

vintage. The year the wine was made.

vintner. The winery owner or a person who sells wine.

viticulture. Grape growing.

Vitis vinifera. The genus and species of Old World grapes used for centuries for fine winemaking.

Wädenswil. A Pinot Noir clone.

Willamette Valley. An Oregon wine region that runs between the Cascade Mountains and the Coast Range from Oregon's northern border to just south of Eugene.

wine thief. Tool that allows the winemaker to take wine from the barrel. See also **thief.**

winemaker. The individual responsible for making the wine. May or may not be the winery owner.

yeasts. The organisms that change sugar to alcohol during fermentation.